Graphic Novel Sketch Book

Create Your own Phenomenal Graphic Novels

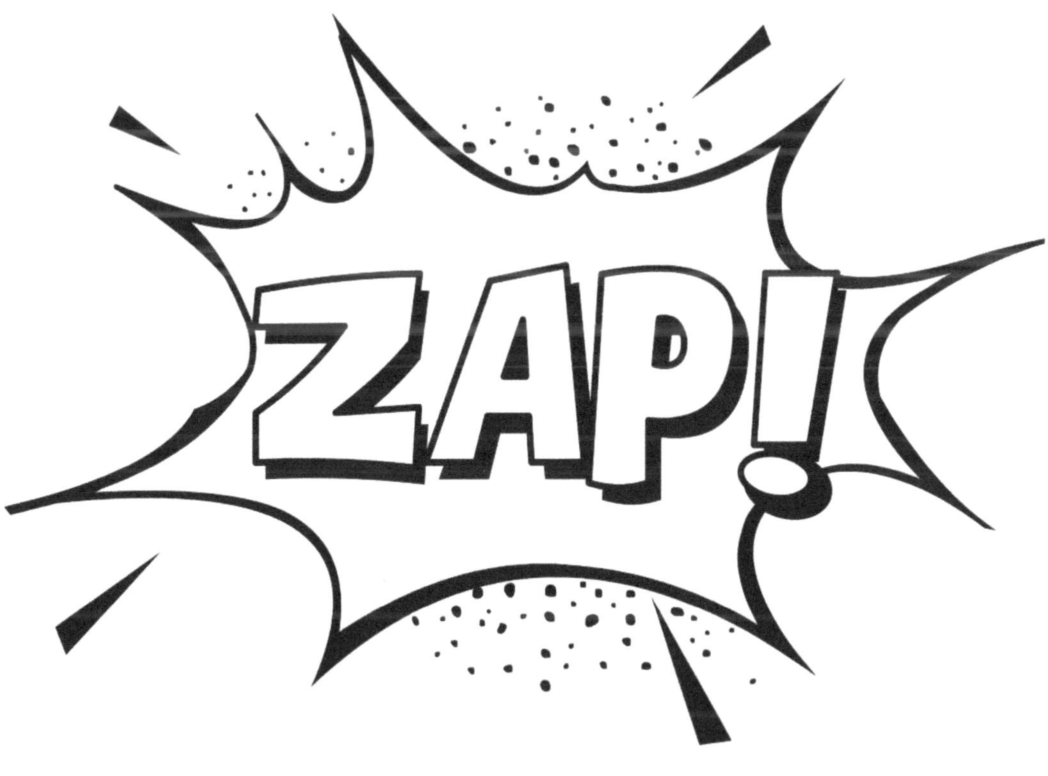

Graphic Novel Sketch Book:

Create Your Own Phenomenal Graphic Novels

Kaye Nutman

First Printing: 2019

ISBN: 13: 978-0-9876404-4-4

OggyTheOggDesign

Brighton Victoria Australia

www.kayenutman-writer.com

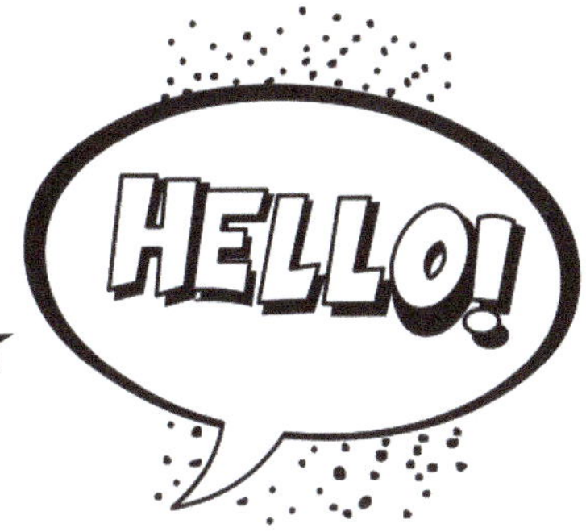

Contents

Welcome!

Reading a graphic novel is like having a printed movie in front of you, so if you love drawing, why not try your hand at a graphic novel? They are lots of fun to do.

The term ***'graphic novel'*** was only coined in 1964 by fan historian, Richard Kyle, who used it in a fanzine. A graphic novel can be full length fiction or non-fiction; it can be an anthology, an adaptation of classic novels, and on any topic under the sun!

There's a difference between a comic and a graphic novel - simply put - a comic can develop a story over many weekly or monthly issues; a graphic novel generally pulls off the whole story in one longer issue (or perhaps two). It can be 20 pages long or it can be over a hundred pages – the great thing is, the choice is up to you!

A graphic novel often has between 5 and 9 panels per page, but smaller panels can be tricky to fill in, so one, or two 'splashes' are sparingly used to emphasise a feature. Most of the templates in this book range from 4 to 7 panels, with a few pages that are splashes of 1,2 or 3 panels.

If you wonder how long it will take you to make a graphic novel then, as the saying goes…"How long is a piece of string?" Even with the story already planned and written, carefully completed art work by professionals could take a year or more!

If you are new to practicing this art form or just want to 'wing it' as you go along and let the art and story develop, keep it simple, then it could be a *much* shorter time. It takes longer if you haven't done the story plot first.

Be careful how many words you fit into your speech bubbles. The rule of thumb is 'no more than you can comfortably fit in', which could be one, five or twenty five. The more panels per page, the fewer words.

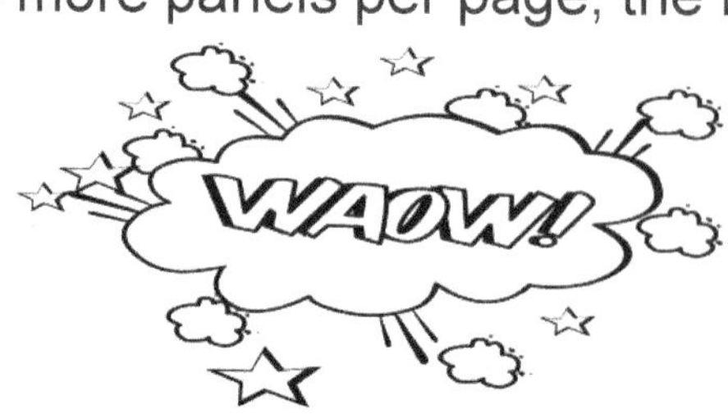

A few Things to Think About

Here are some things you should consider if you want to start drawing your own graphic novel. If you just start off drawing you might run out of ideas – so it's best to plan ahead.

What's the Theme of Your Graphic Novel?

Think about what kind of graphic novel you want it to be. What's it going to be about? Is it an everyday slice of life or the biography of a famous astronaut? Aliens, zombies or dragons? Comedy or action and adventure? Steampunk or rap and hip hop or a Christian tale? Formula 1 Grand Prix, soccer or secret agents? Things like this are important!

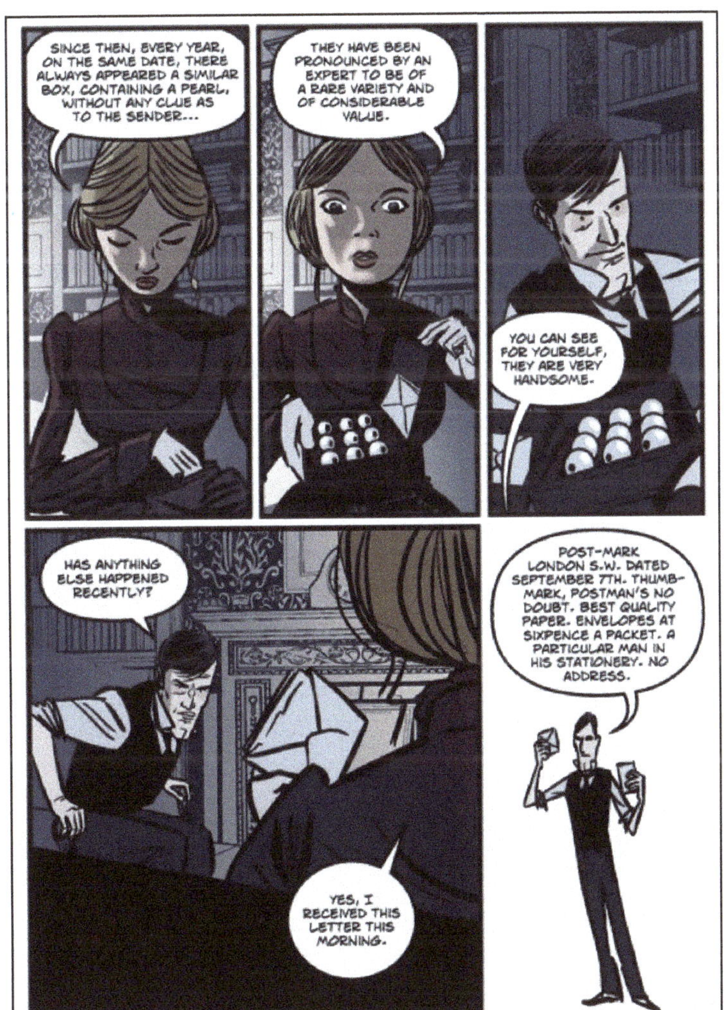

Who are your Characters?

You need at least one main character and maybe a couple of supporting characters. Think about the personality of each. Who is the star? Who are his/her friends... or enemies? Make them unique from each other. You do not really have to create a long list of characters, and can add another in later. Remember, they don't have to be human *or* animal!

Expressions

Practice... Try out some facial expressions for your characters. Can you make a face look - worried, cheeky, laughing, winking, angry and so on? There are plenty of pages at the beginning of this book where you can do just that. Here are a few ideas for actions and expressions. Could take them from the alien and add them to your characters?

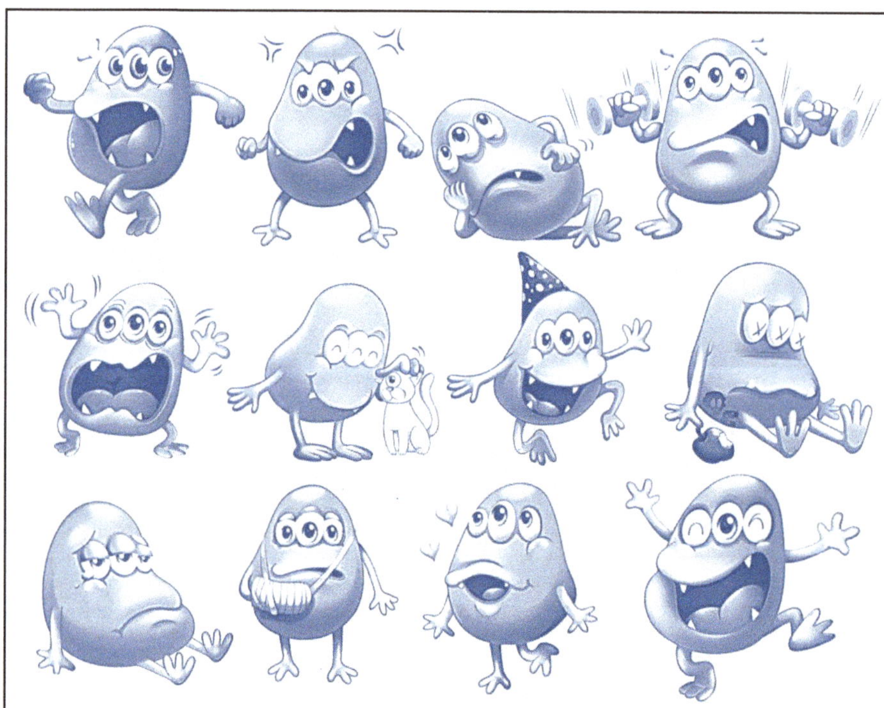

Think of A Setting

Decide on a setting. Will it be during the Jurassic age like in The Flintstones? Would you want it to be set in a high school? Do you want to have your own imaginary city like Gotham city in the Batman comics? Once you have all these things settled in your mind, then it's time to start drawing. It may be best to start with a pencil, then move on to inking the outline and colouring in.

Create a Storyboard

Once you have a story theme worked out in your head you can create a few simple storyboards. This is a set of basic line drawings illustrating how you want the finished artwork to look. It doesn't have to be pretty! You can refer to it for the basic flow of the story. Think of the plot for the scenes on each page, along with the words you have in mind.

Speech Bubbles

Think... Where will you use speech bubbles?
These are the shapes that can contain expressions like Wow! Yes! Or sounds like Bang! And of course, Speech!
To whisper or think you could use dotted lines. To shout or for loud noises, use spiky lines.
You can add dots, shading and extra drawing bits, like hearts or stars.
At the back of this book you will find a selection of Speech bubbles to cut out and stick in. or copy.

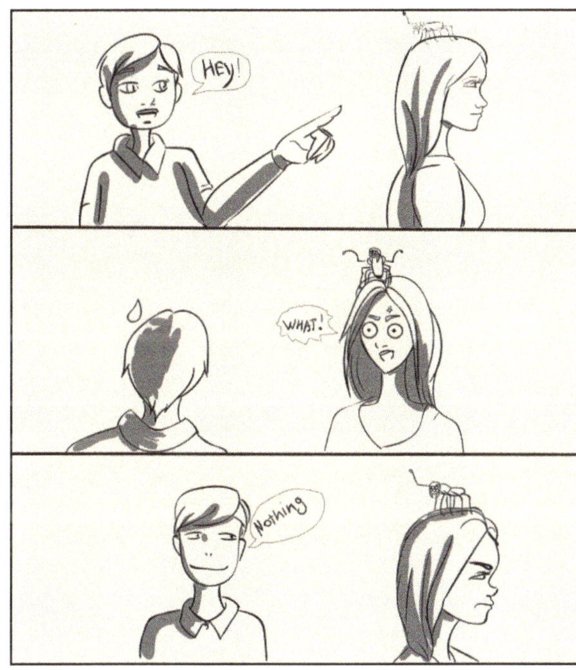

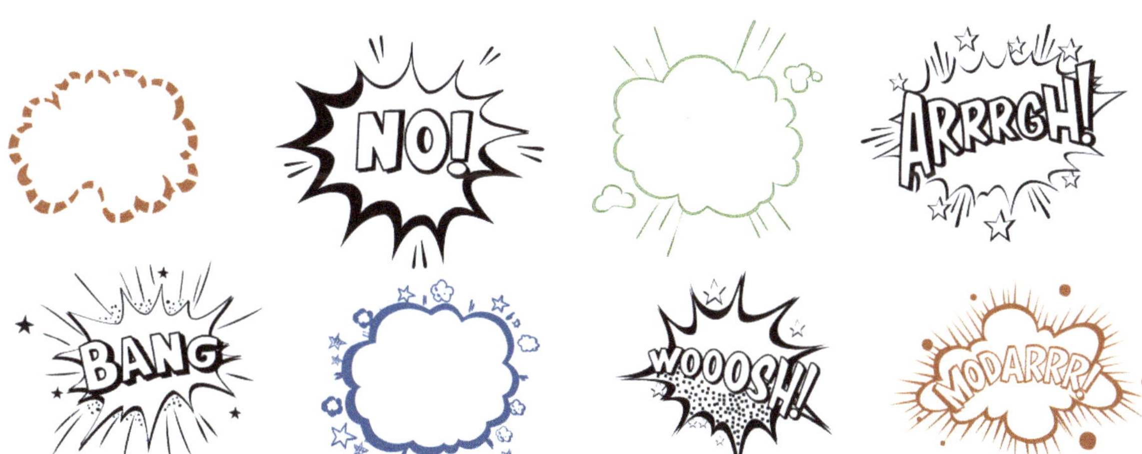

Start working out how you are going to fit your characters in the boxes and then draw them. Put in speech bubbles or dialogue boxes and write in their words or thoughts. If a panel is small use it for faces or just upper or lower body. If it's large use it for a whole scene, like a village view and so on. If the boxes slant or have an indentation, work out how you can use that to make the scene look good.

Exaggerate!

You can show crucial parts in your story by using exaggeration. Zoom in on a certain object – try a foot hitting the ball; a shouting mouth. Change the perspective – look down or from a distance getting closer. Change colours – an angry face getting red; big grey clouds. Add effects like weather and shadow – make a face look scary!

Lastly

Once you are happy with your idea, draw it onto a set of panels in pencil, then ink the outlines in and erase the sketch marks. Add some shading and color if you want to, and... you're done! Some of the layouts in this book are -

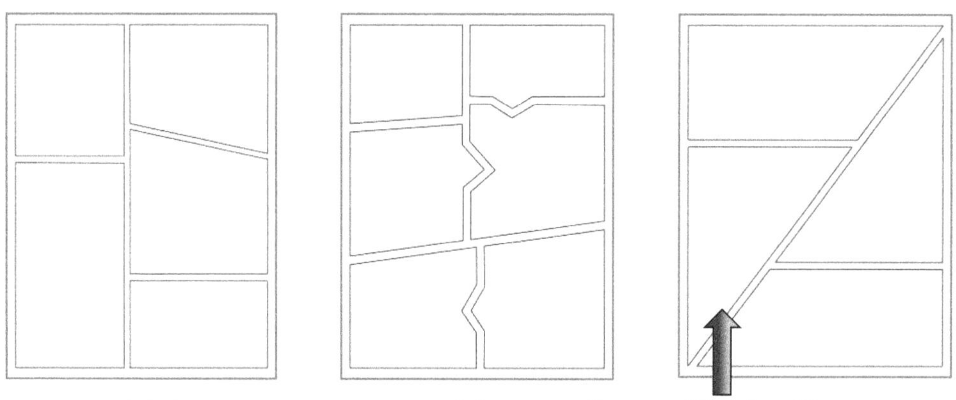

It's up to you which way up you want to use them. **Portrait** or **Landscape**? Whichever suits your novel best, but use it consistently.

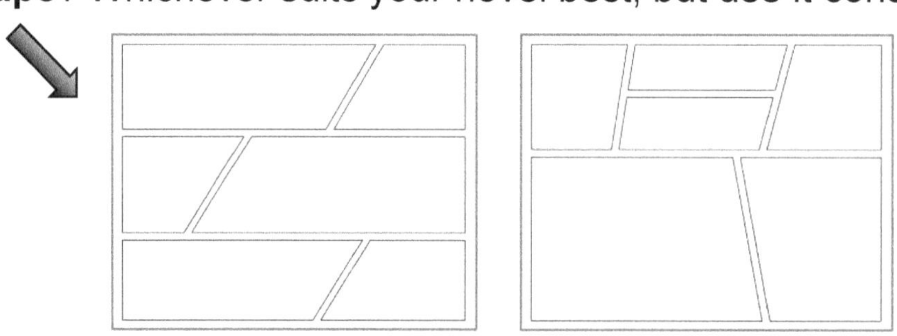

Don't Forget...

LEARN... How? Look at graphic novels and see how they are made up. Perhaps you could join a Cartoon School in the holidays? Or find a great book that teaches graphic novel designing and making - I bet the library has some! Or do an online course?

Graphic novel drawing is lots of FUN both for professionals who earn their living through it and hobbyists who draw for pleasure. I do not know what your goal is, but hope these few tips will be helpful for you. Never stop learning!

Have fun!

This is your book.

Page Titles are just suggestions.

Use it any way you like! Use as many pages as YOU want for your story, or use every page for a longer graphic novel.

The choice is yours.

Please note: The first part of this book is designed so that you gain a little insight into what it takes to put together a graphic novel, and so you can practice drawing. The paper in this book is high quality #60 or 70lb (100gsm or 105gsm), so colours should not bleed through to the other side – but try your coloured pens here first!

Permanent markers =

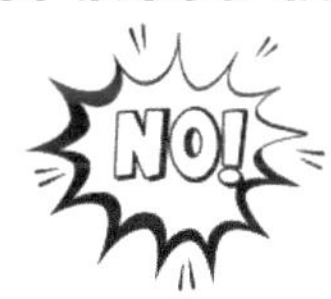

There are 30 unique templates. The majority of the book is made up of these varied templates mixed together over 90 pages of 3 – 7 panels. There's room along the inner margin to comfortably draw or score a line and cut the pages out. They can then be stapled together outside the book. You don't have to do it this way - just draw to your heart's content!

Practice Your Character Drawing

Have a go at this character, then try some more!

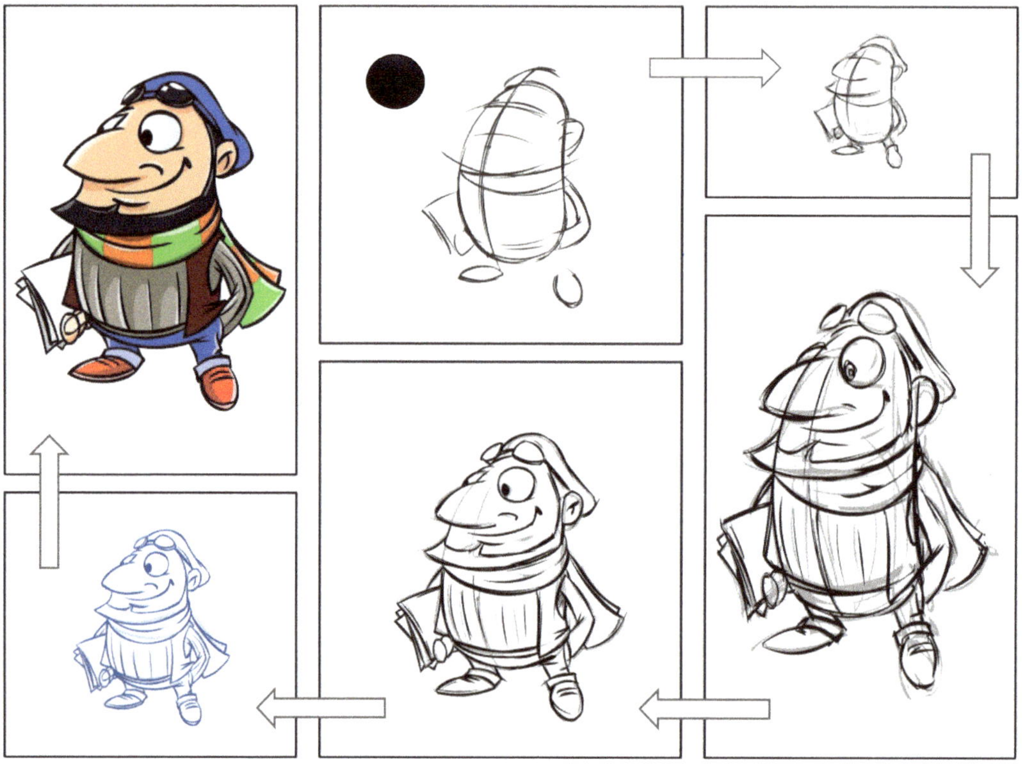

Sketch Pages

Use the sketch pages to

- Practice drawing characters and settings
- Copy one of the trickier box shapes from a panel
- Fit your drawing in
- Plot out a story board
- Practice drawing Speech Bubbles
- Write the words you want to use
- Work out the size you need a speech bubble to be
- Draw your own Graphic Novel templates
- Anything else you desire!

Sketch Page

Sketch Page

Sketch Page

Sketch Page

Sketch Page

Sketch Page

Sketch Page

Sketch Page

Sketch Page

Cover Page for your Graphic Novel

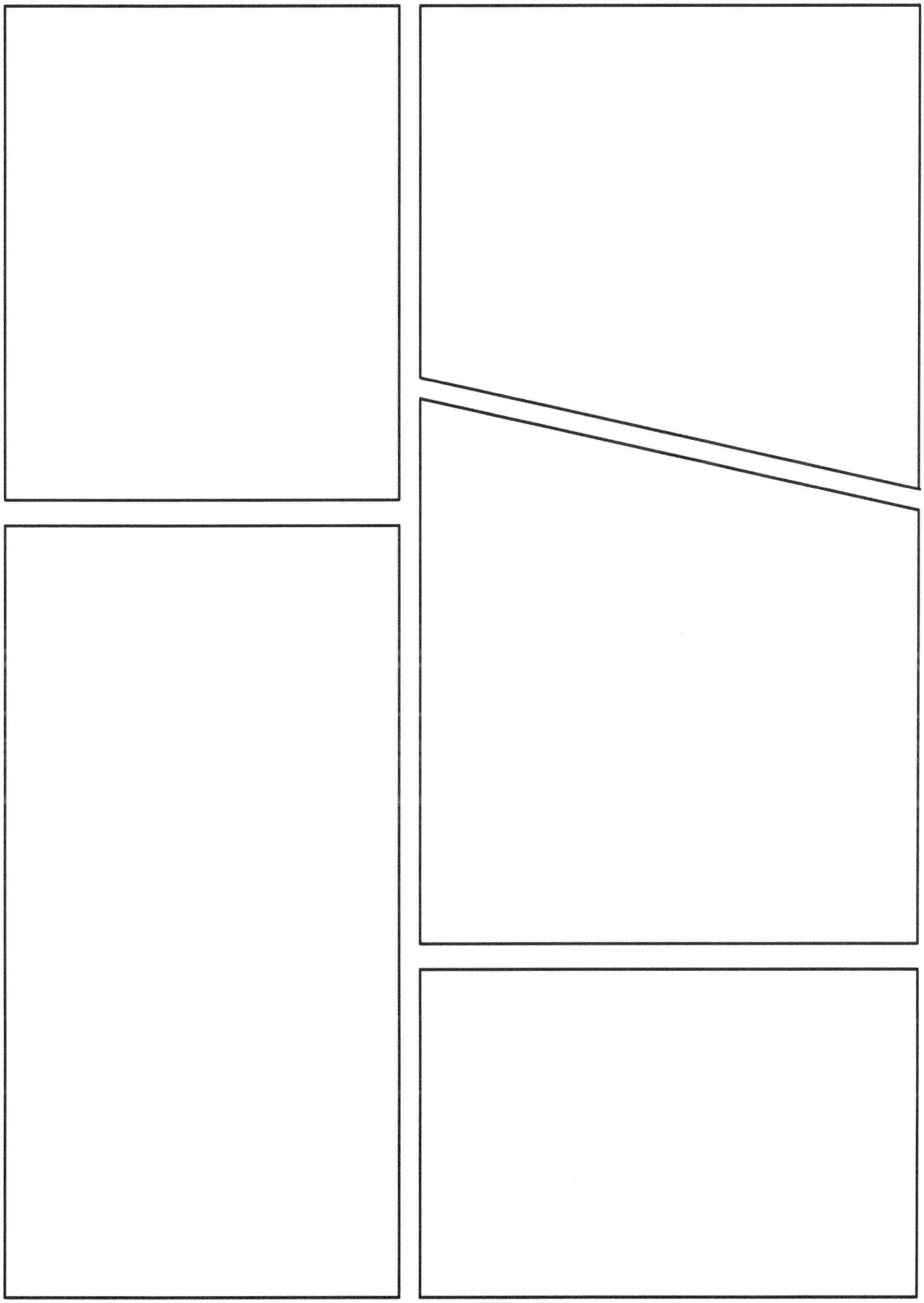

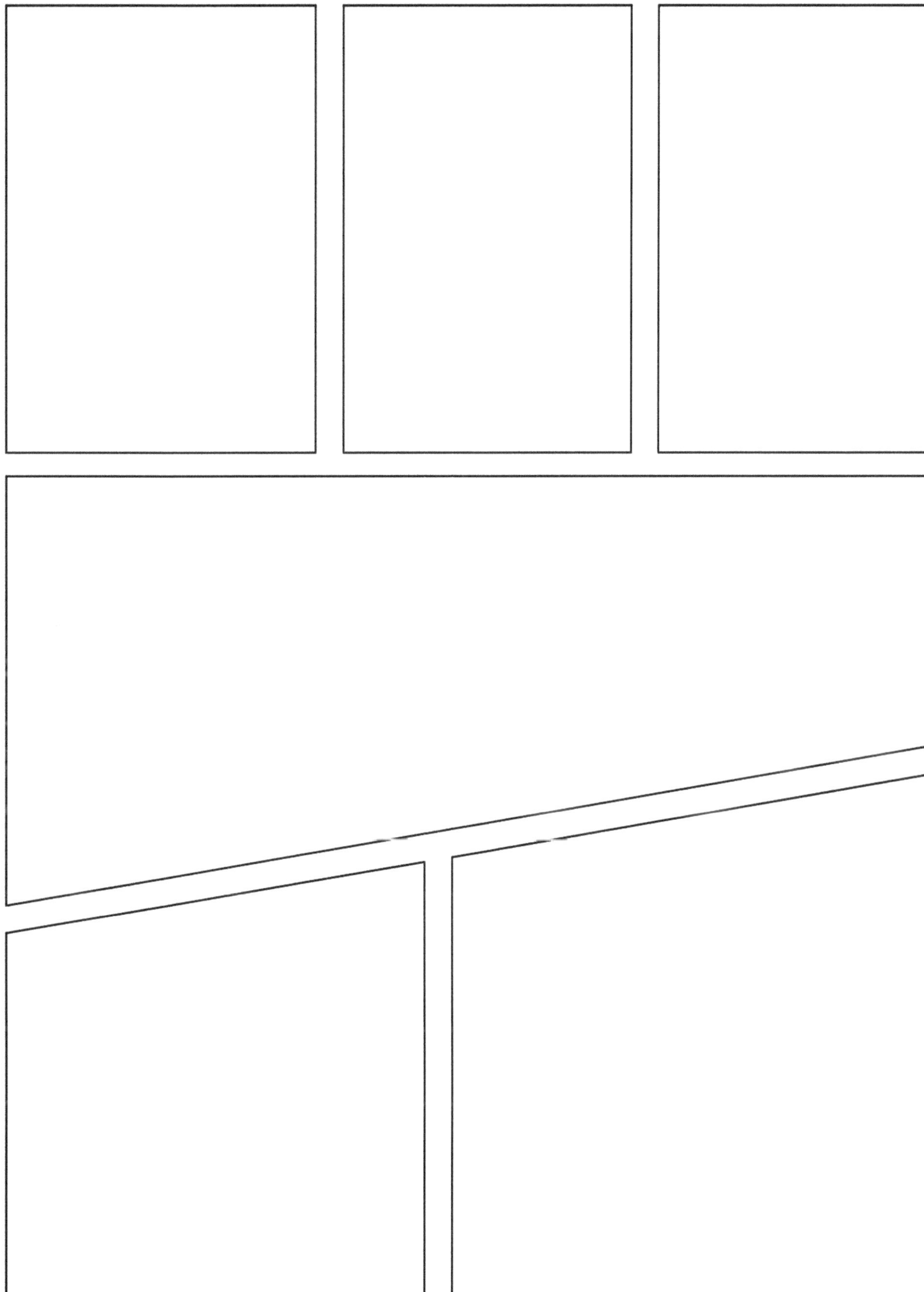

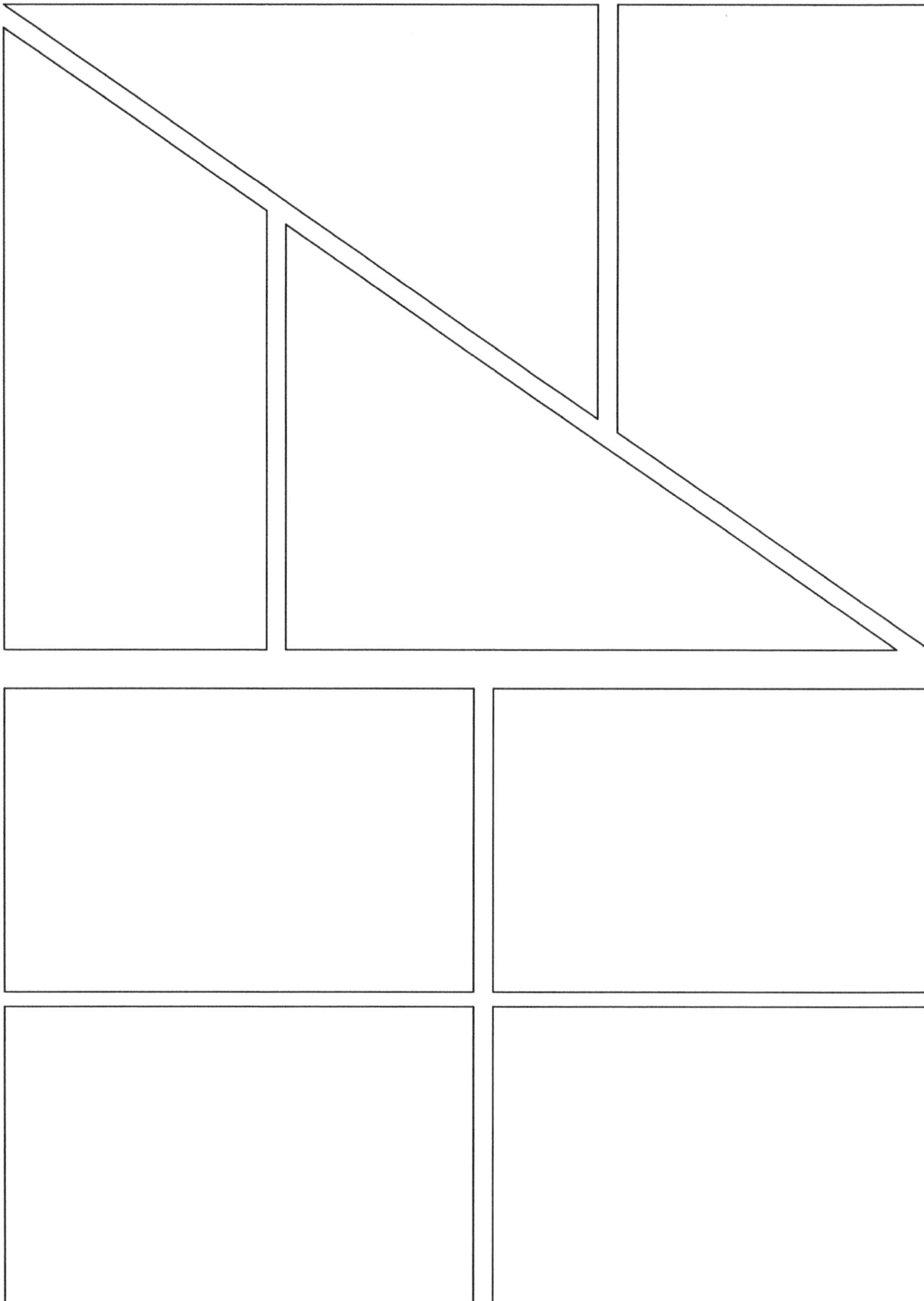

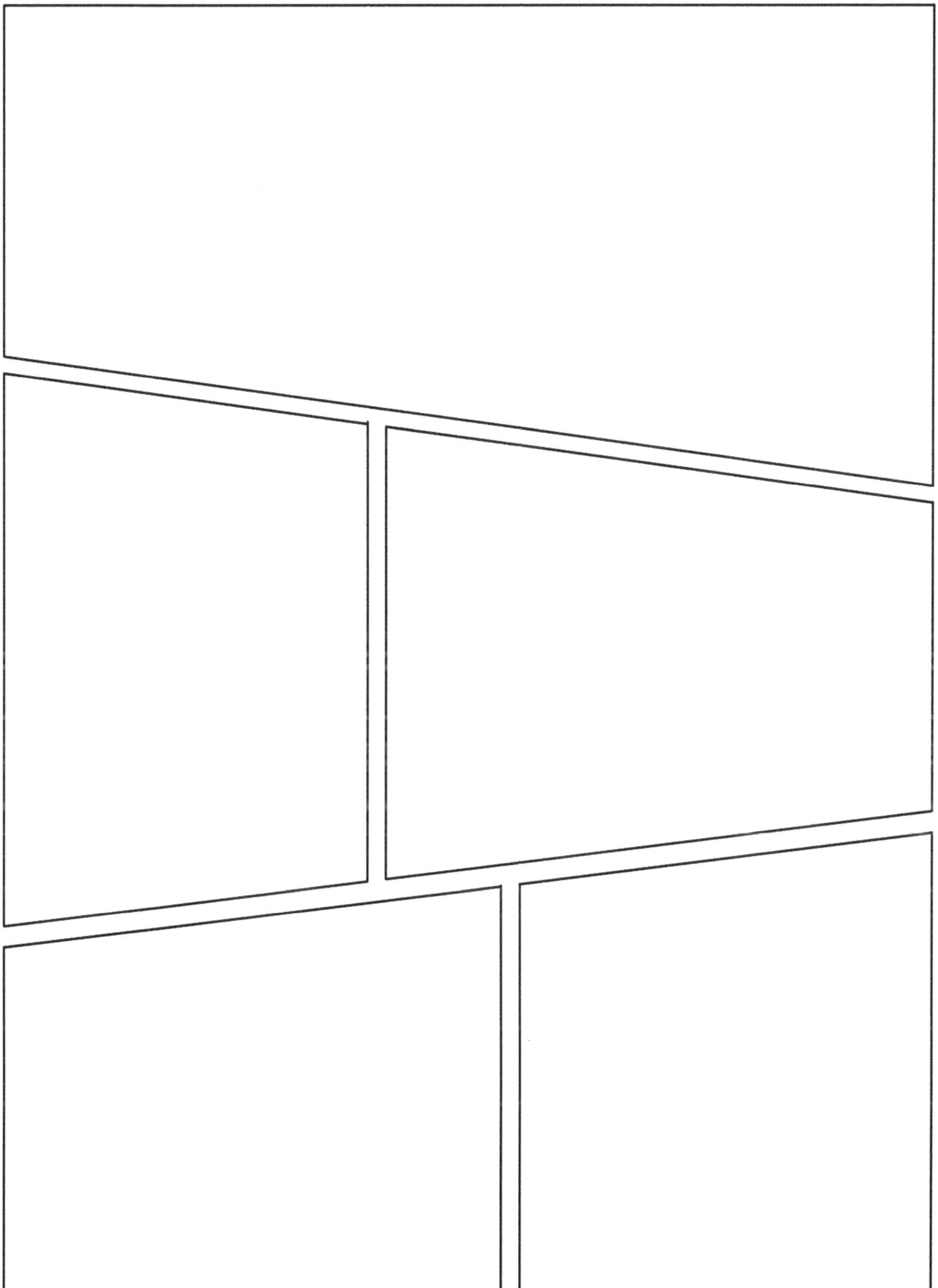

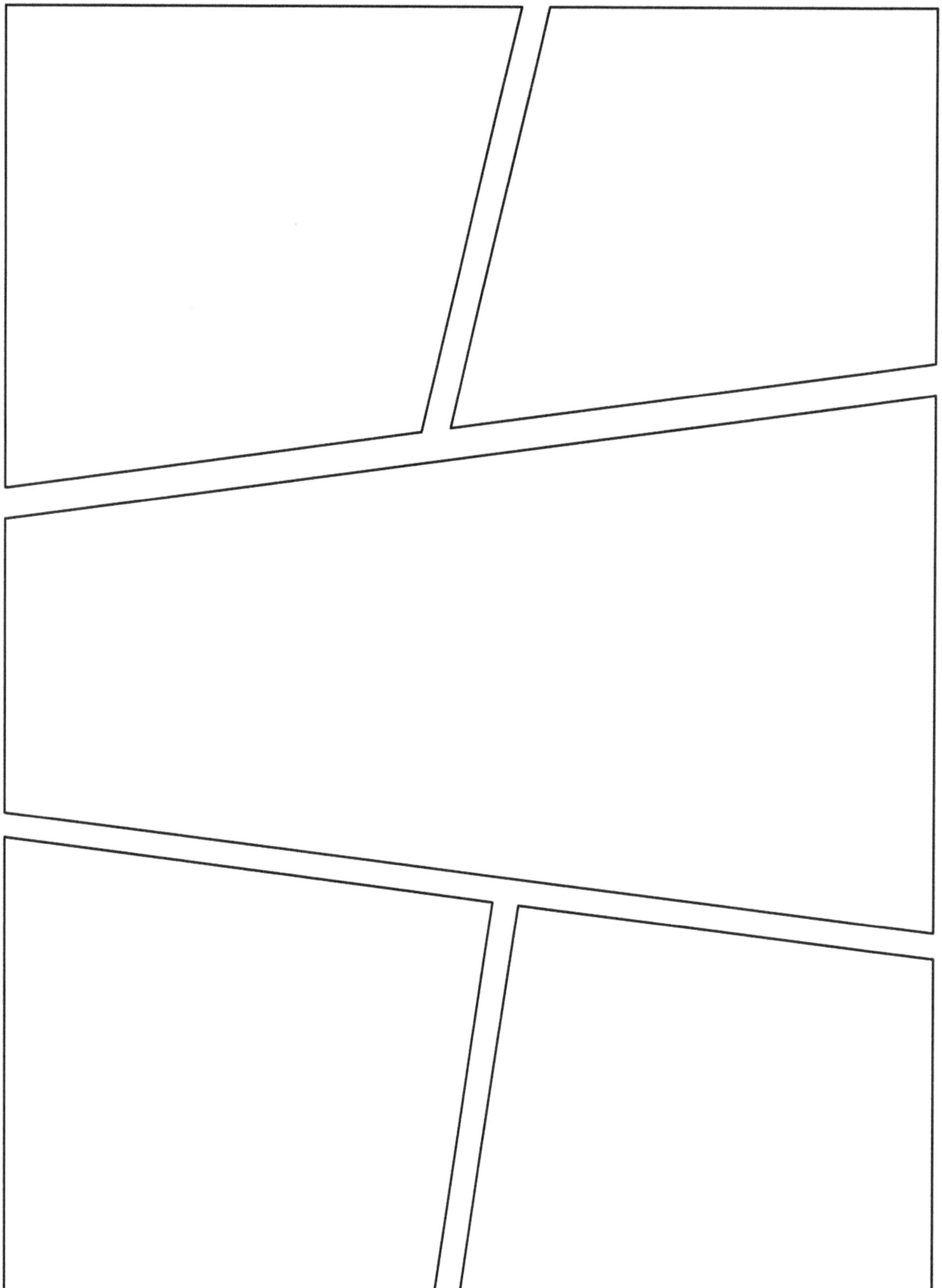

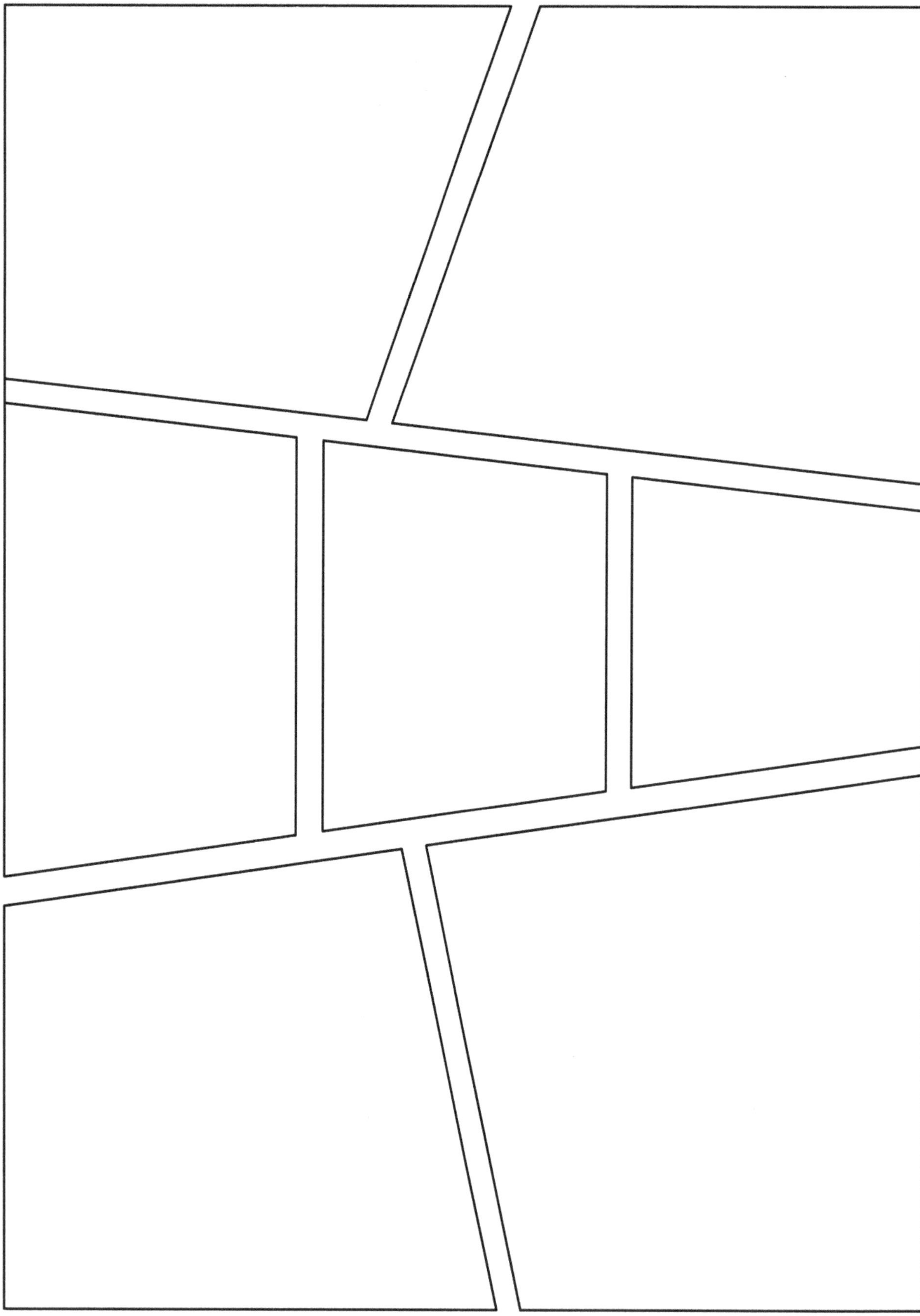

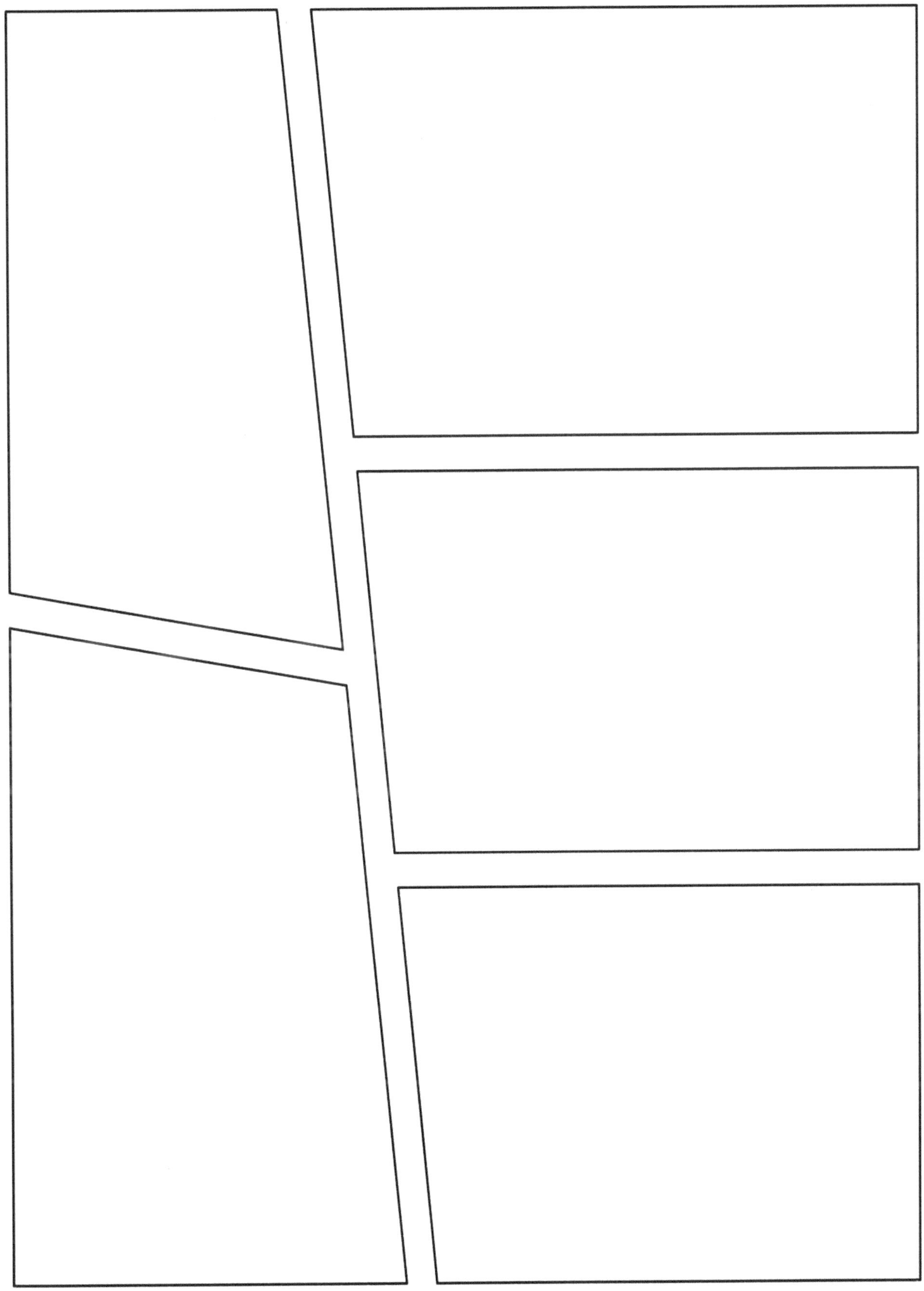

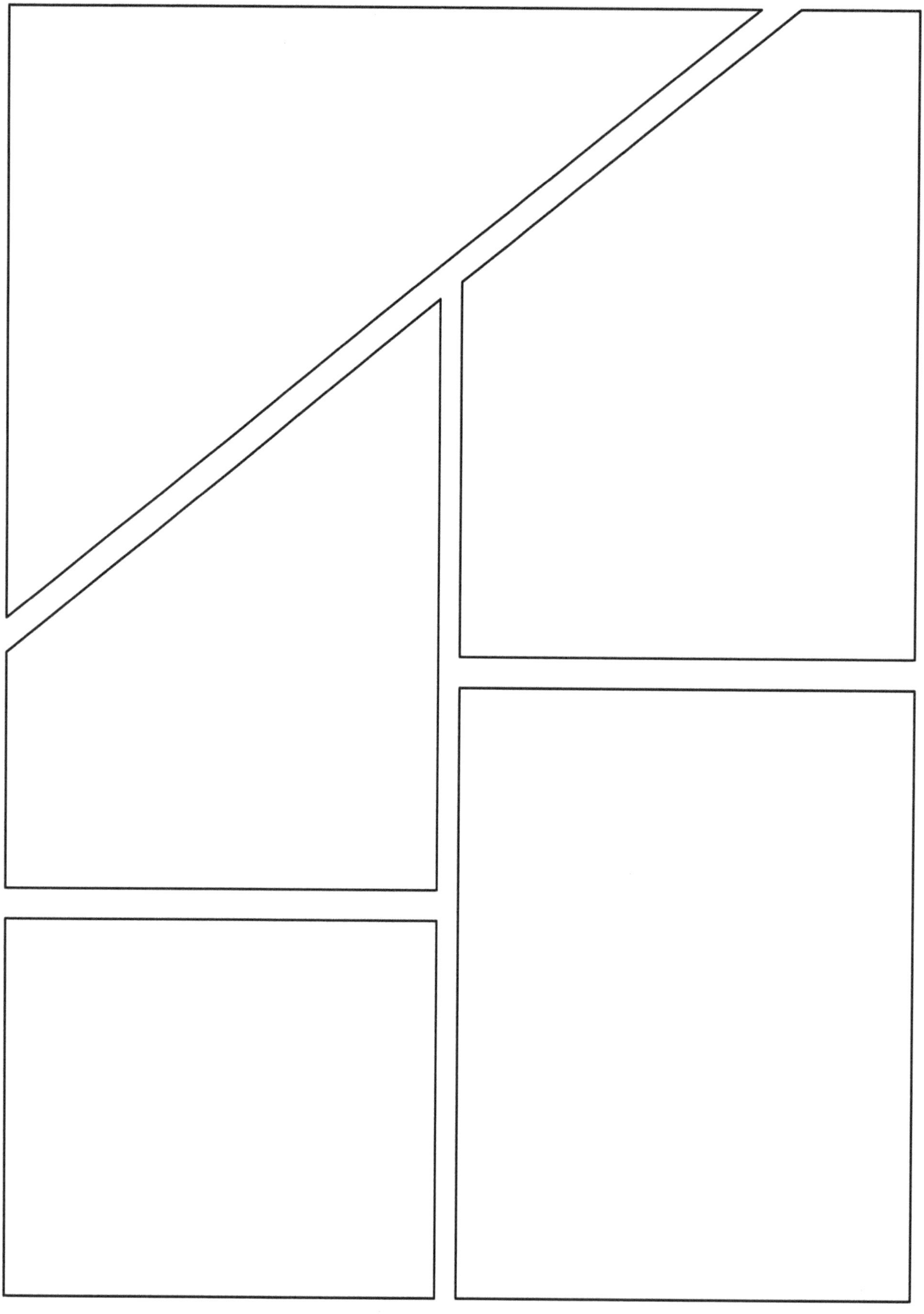

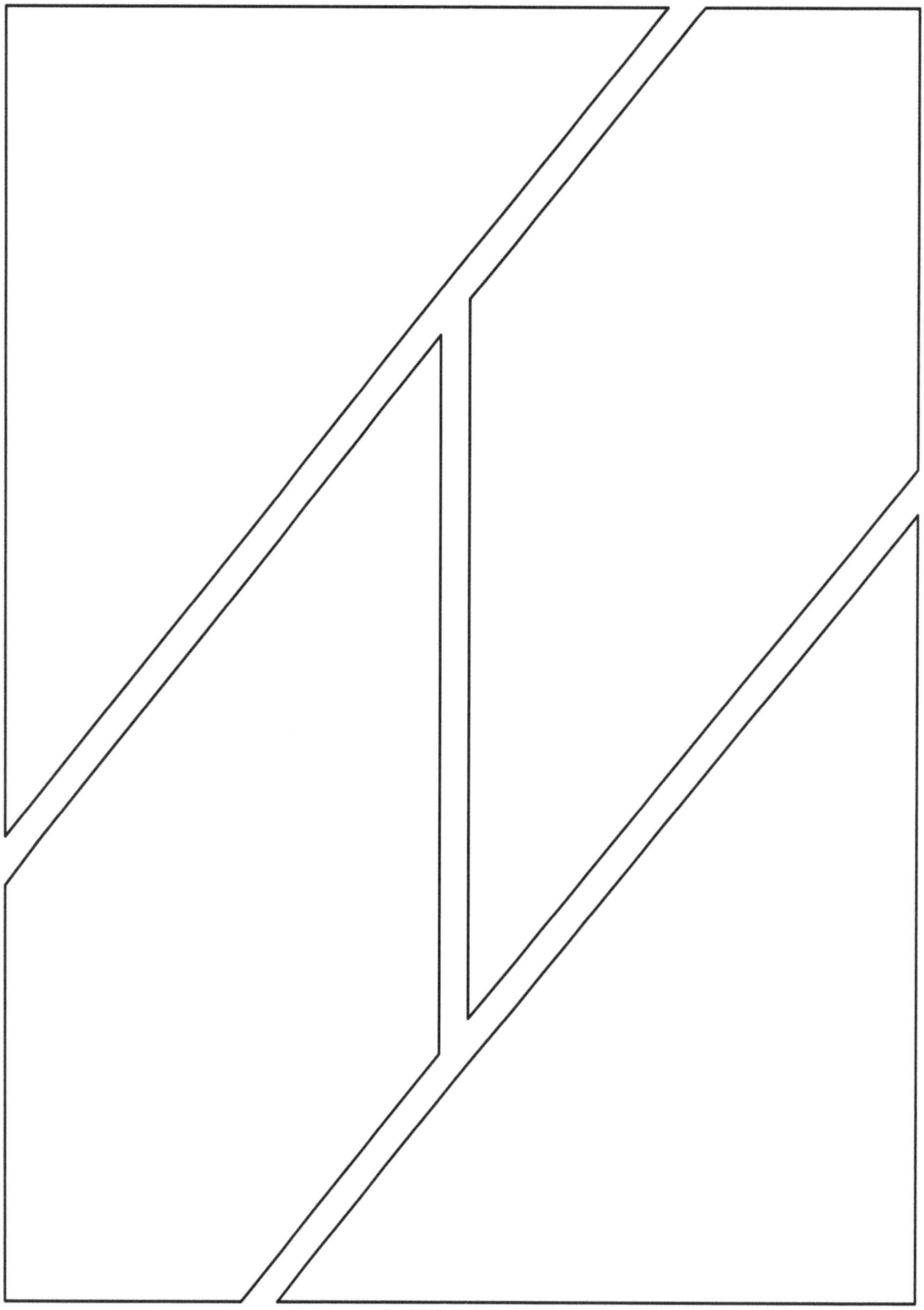

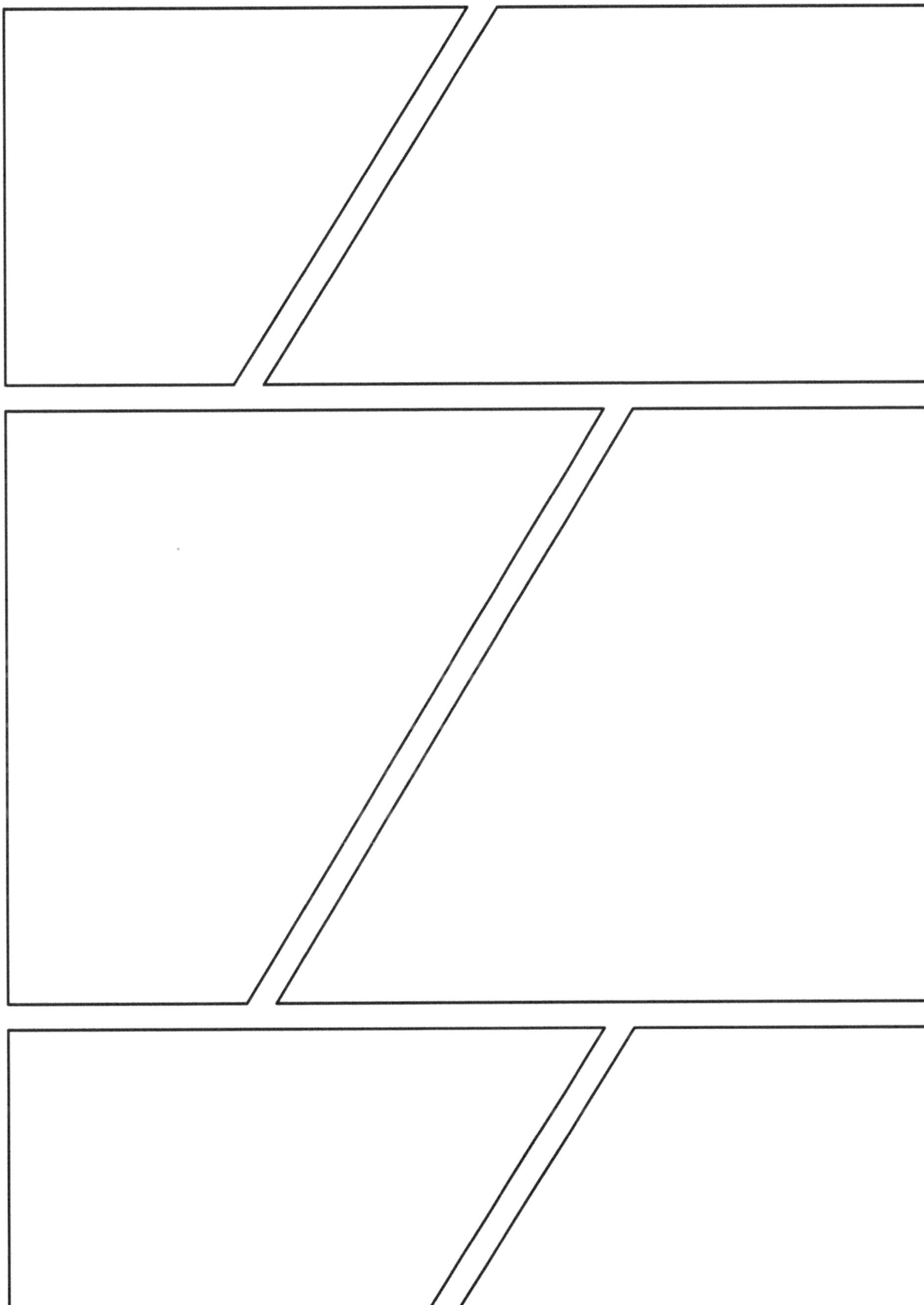

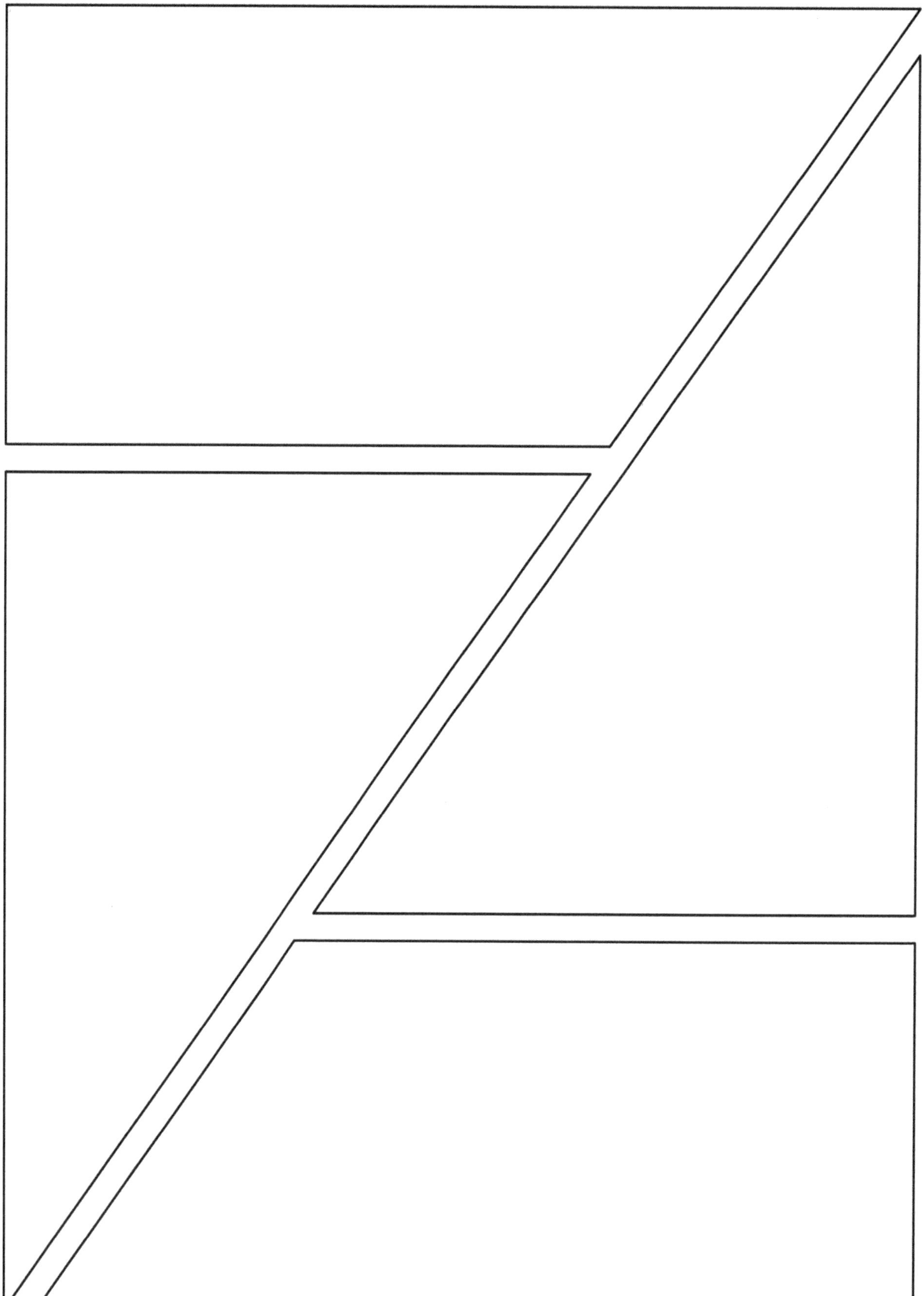

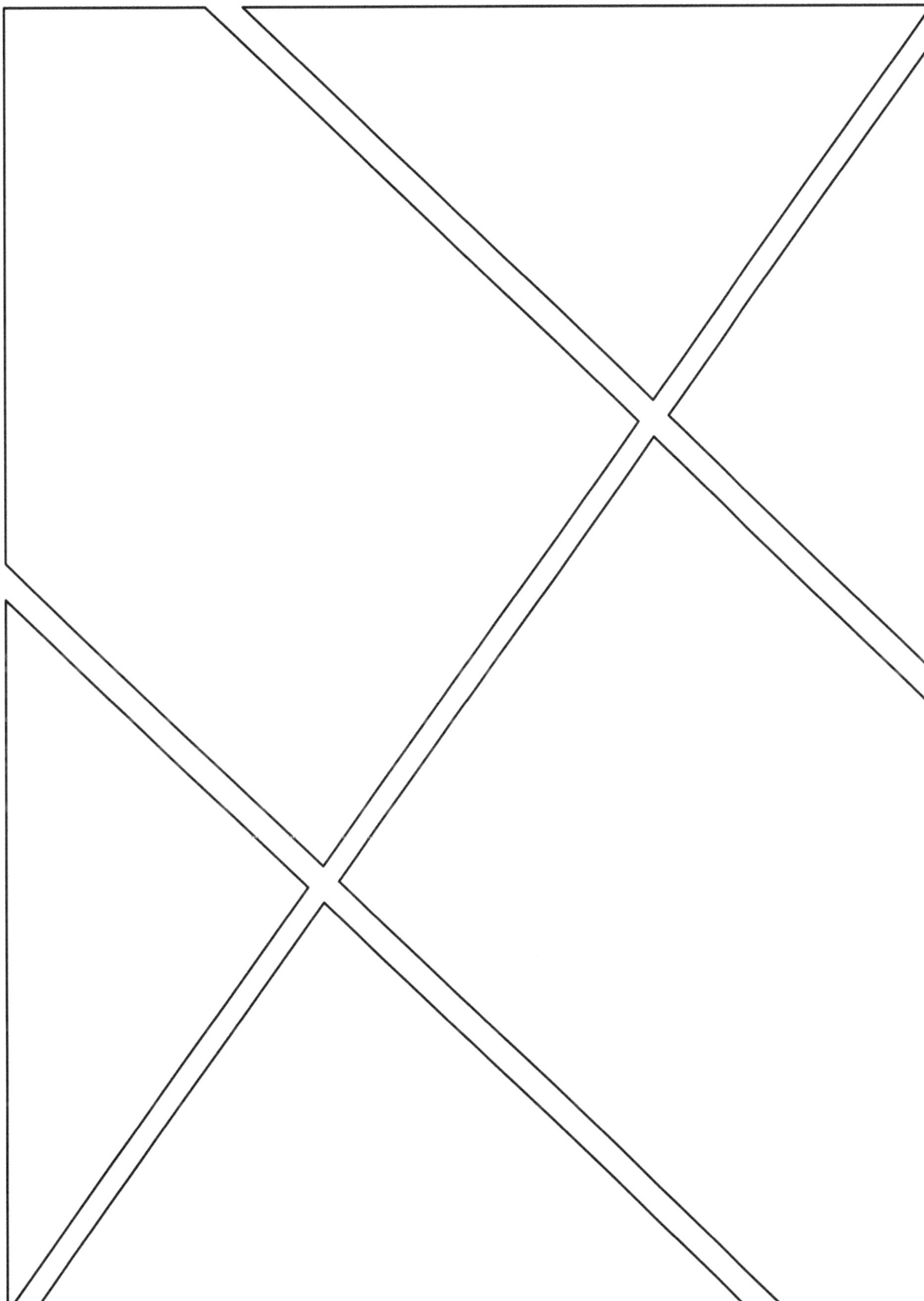

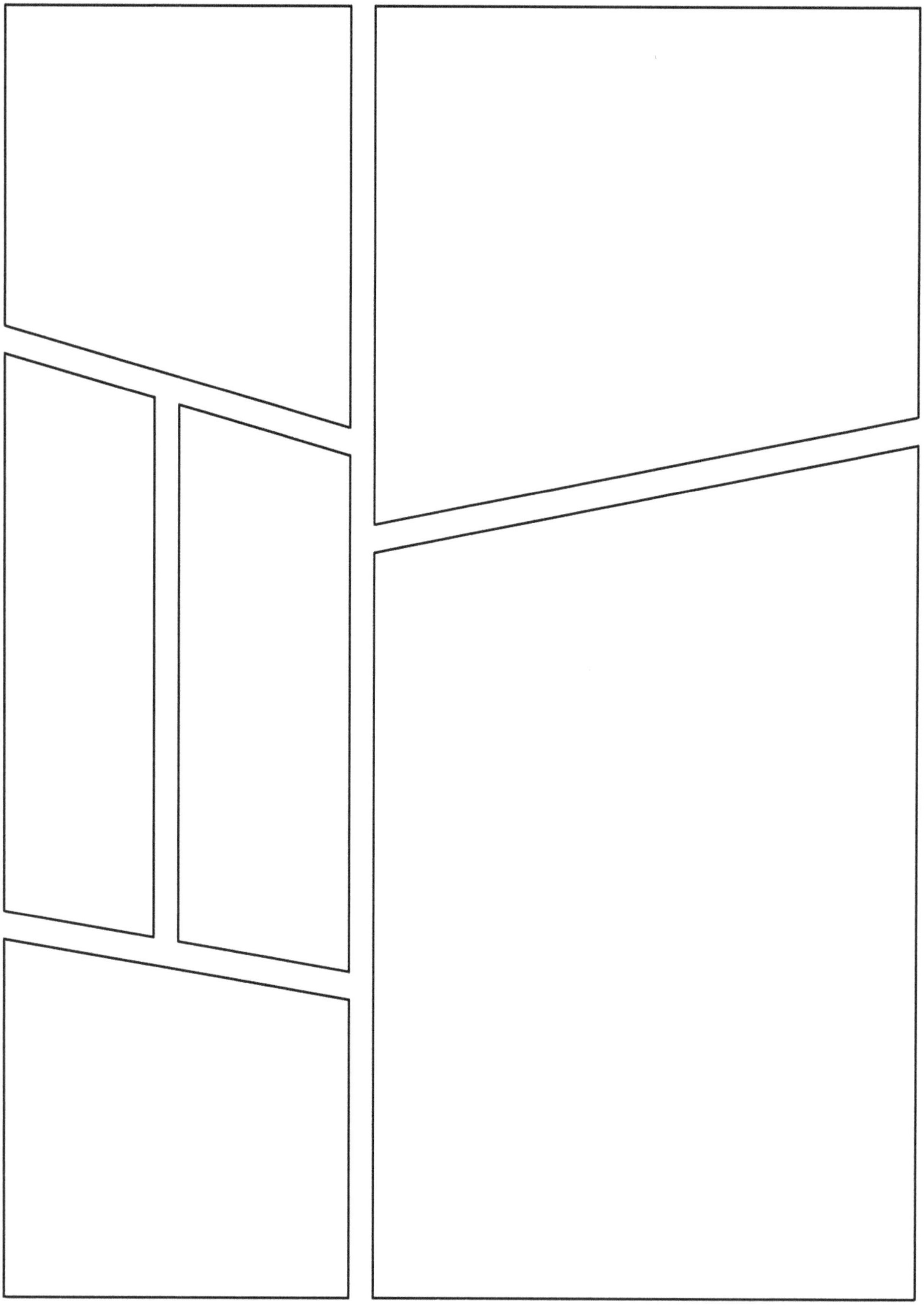

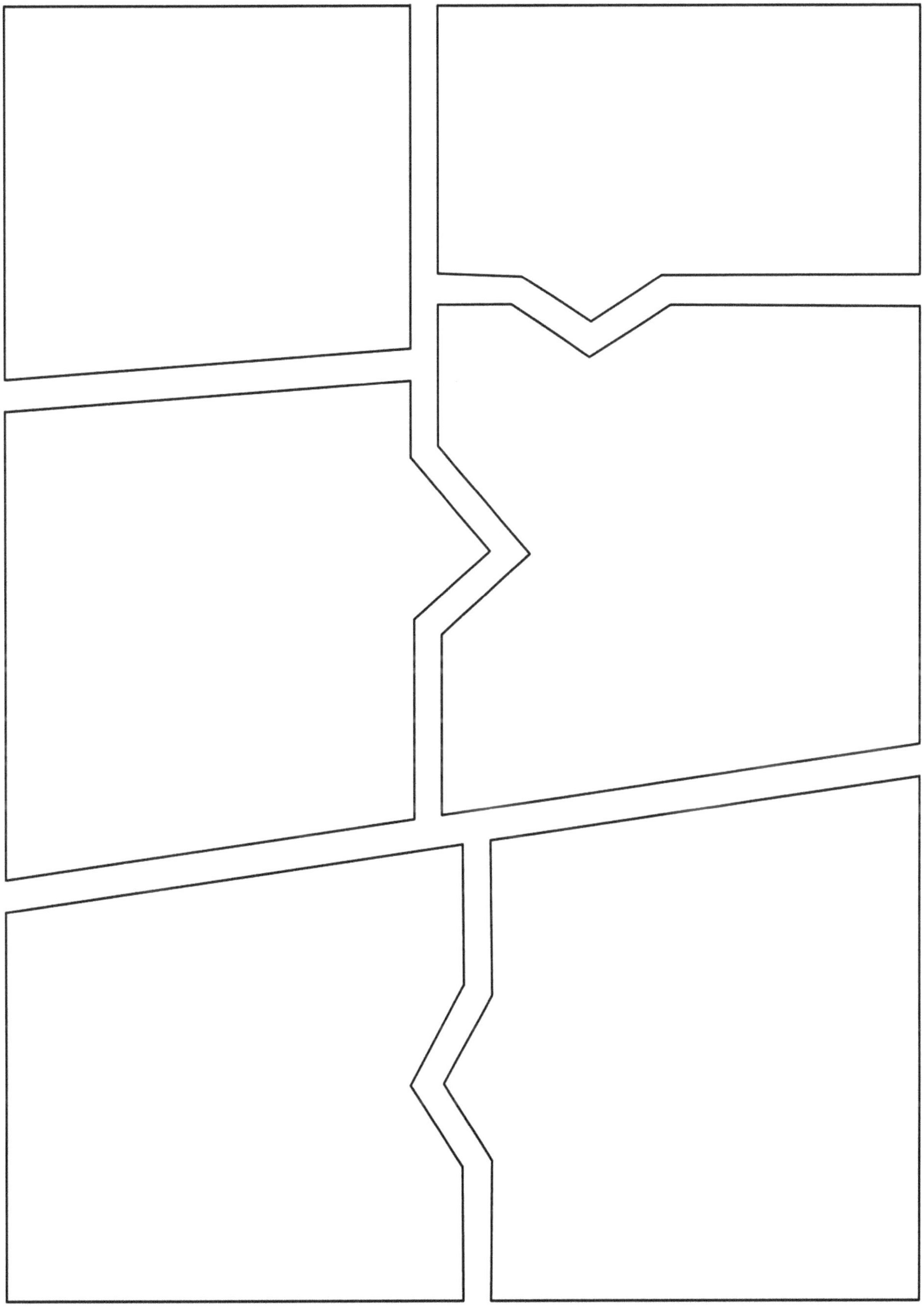

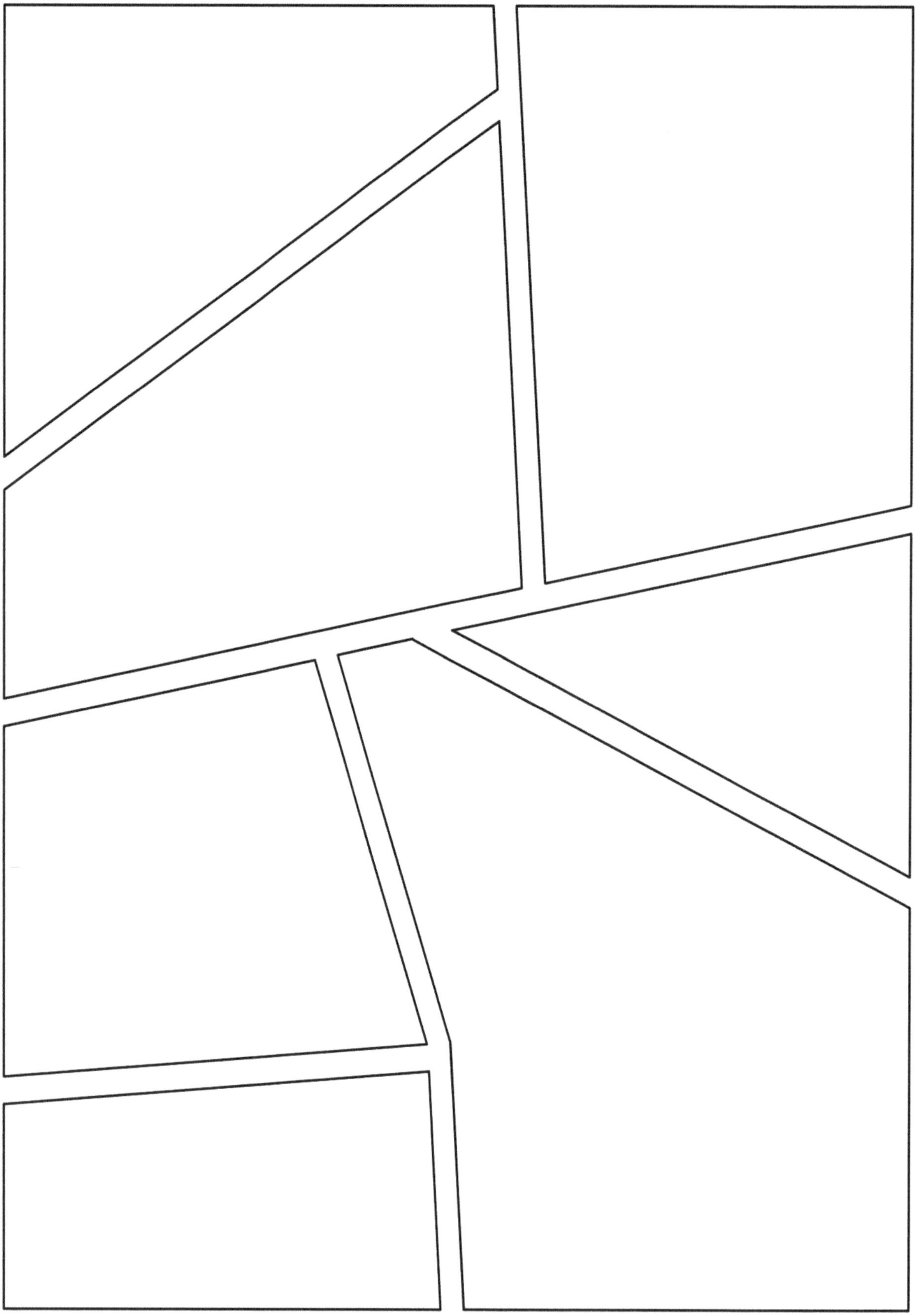

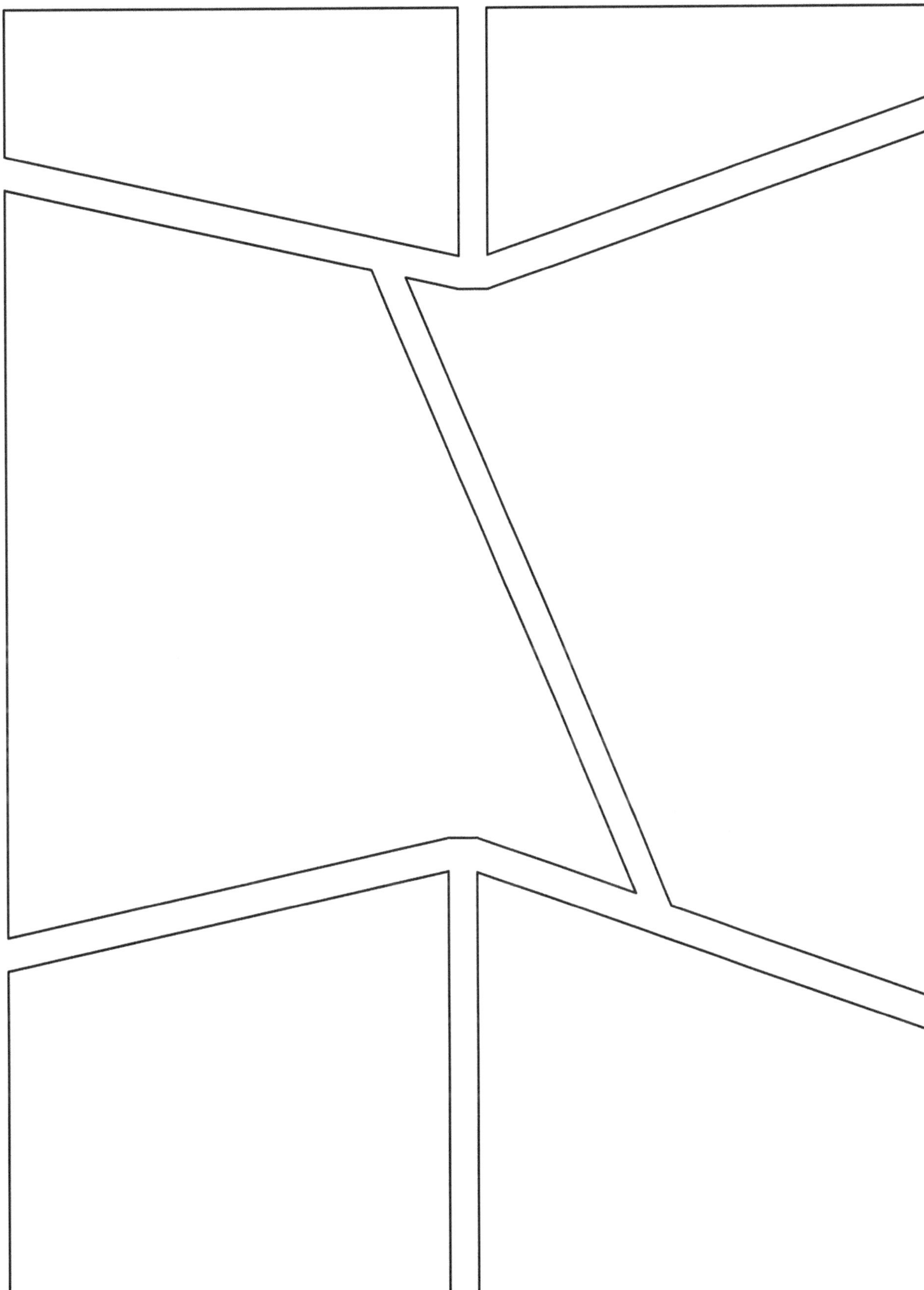

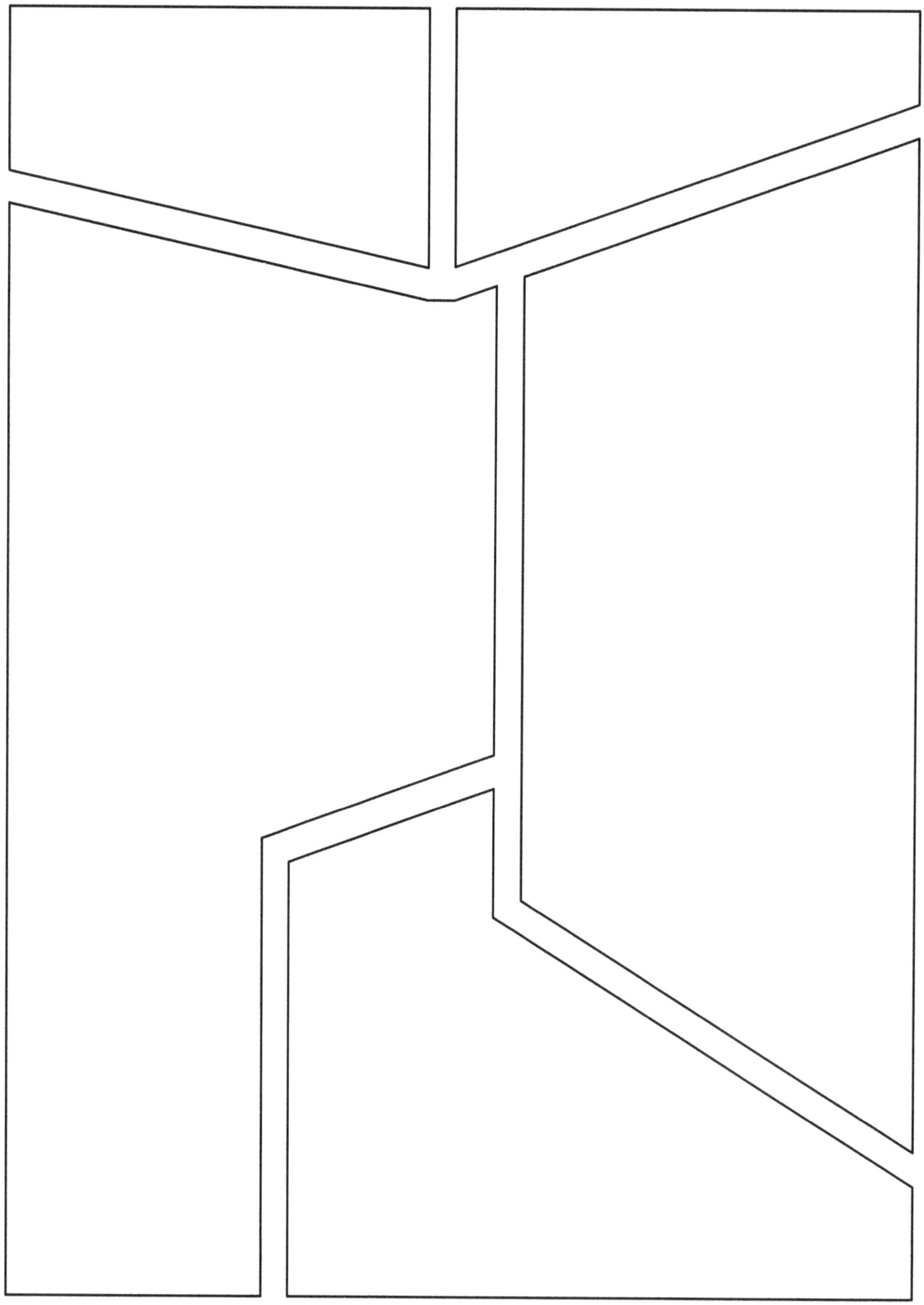

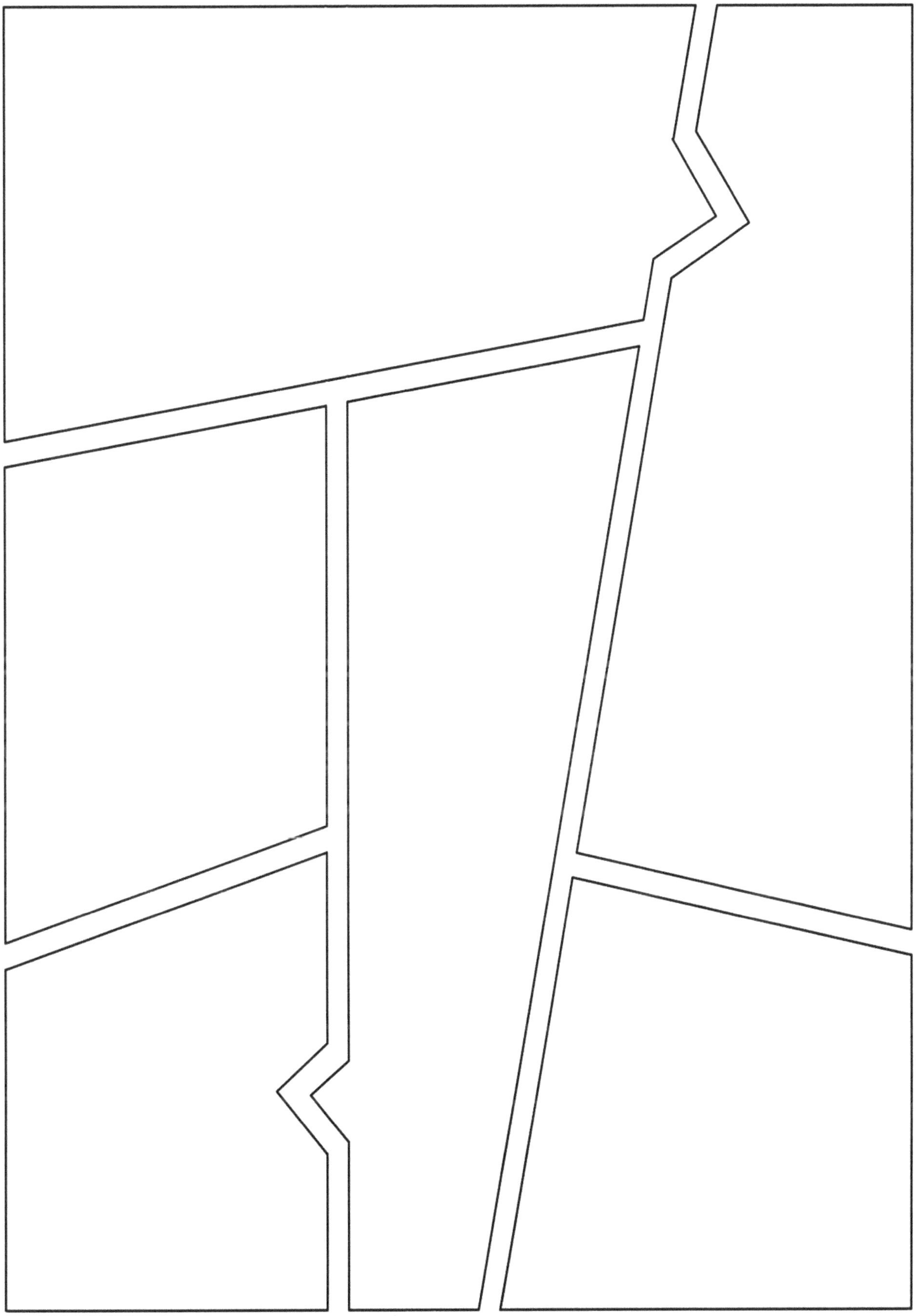

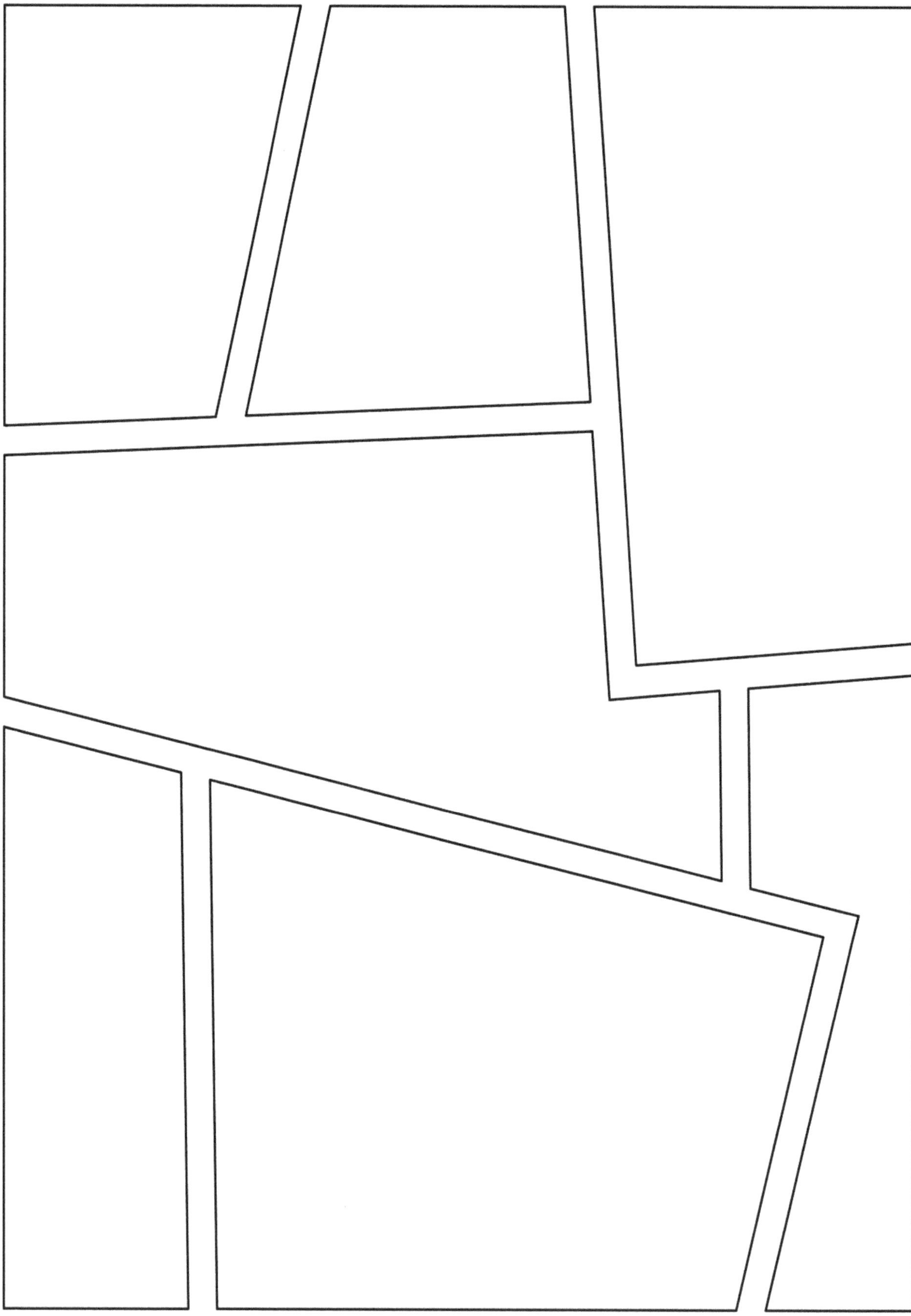

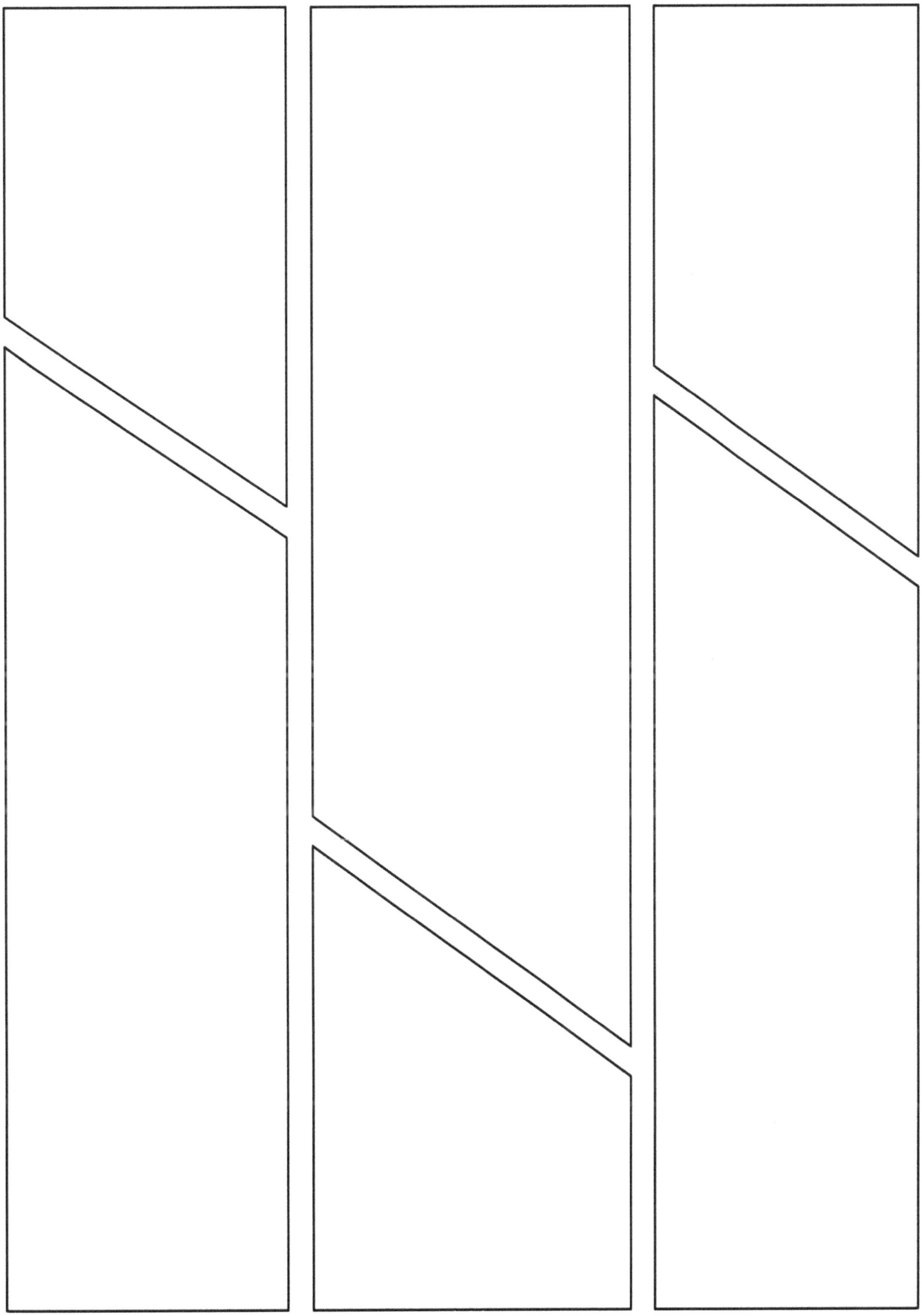

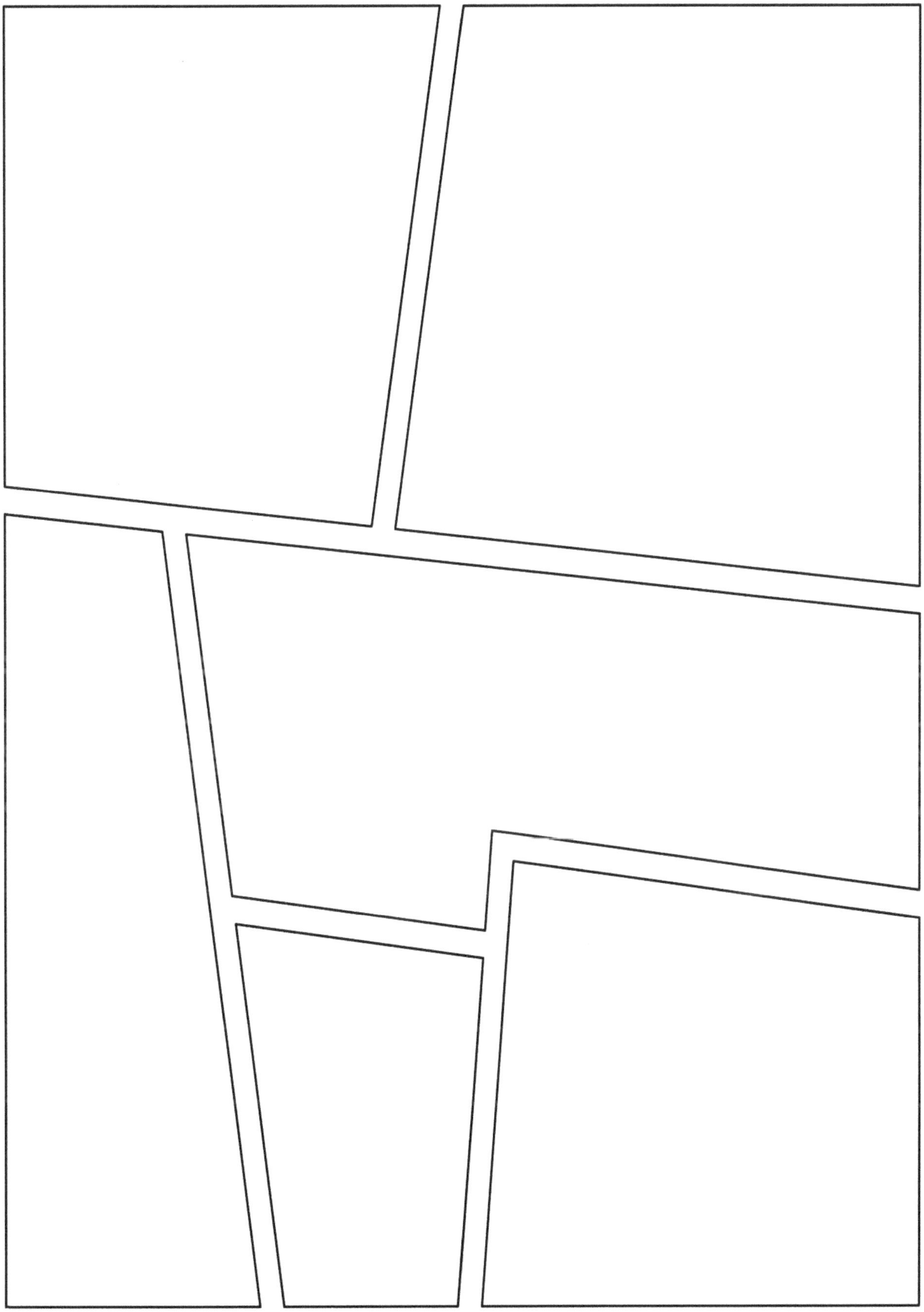

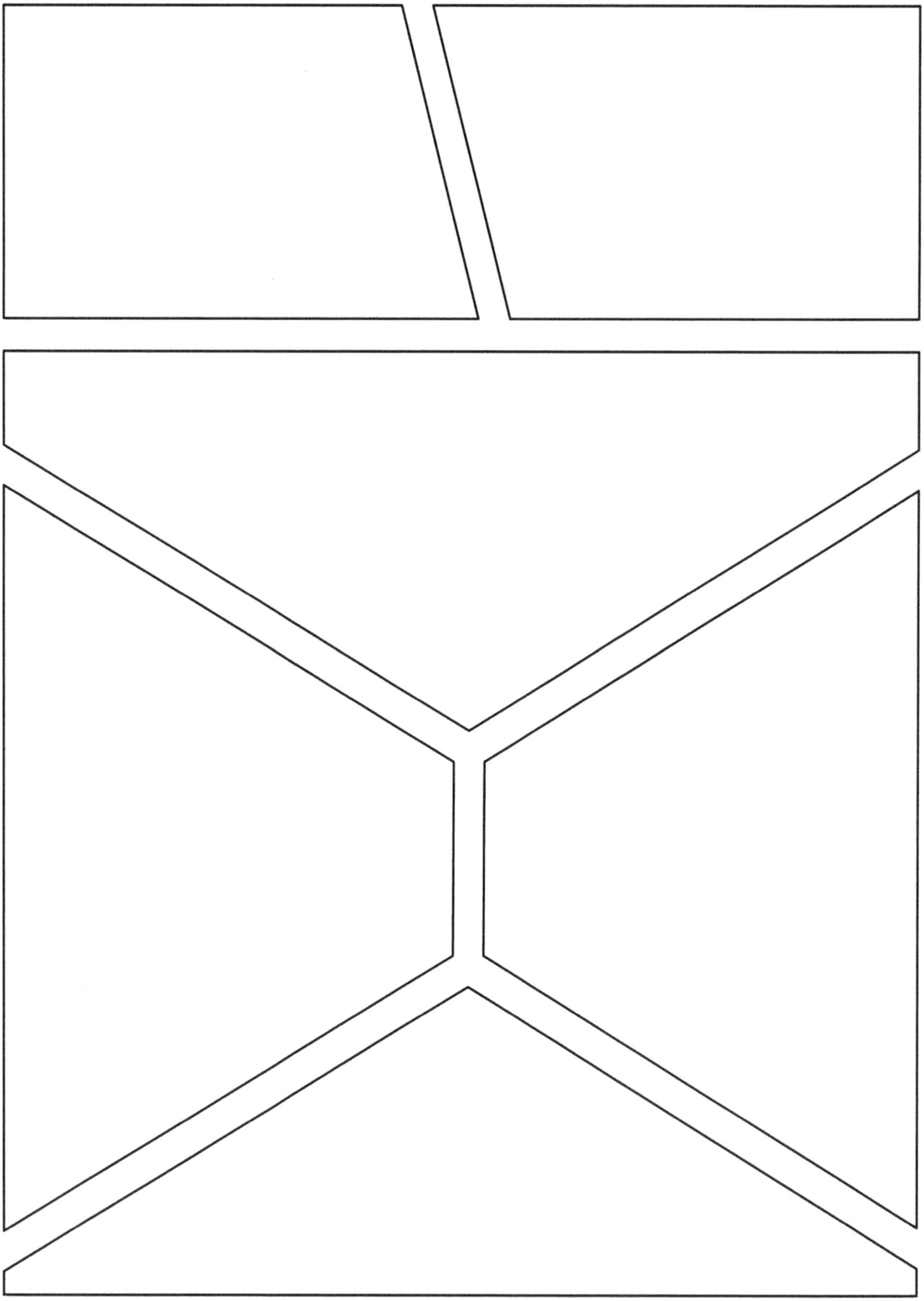

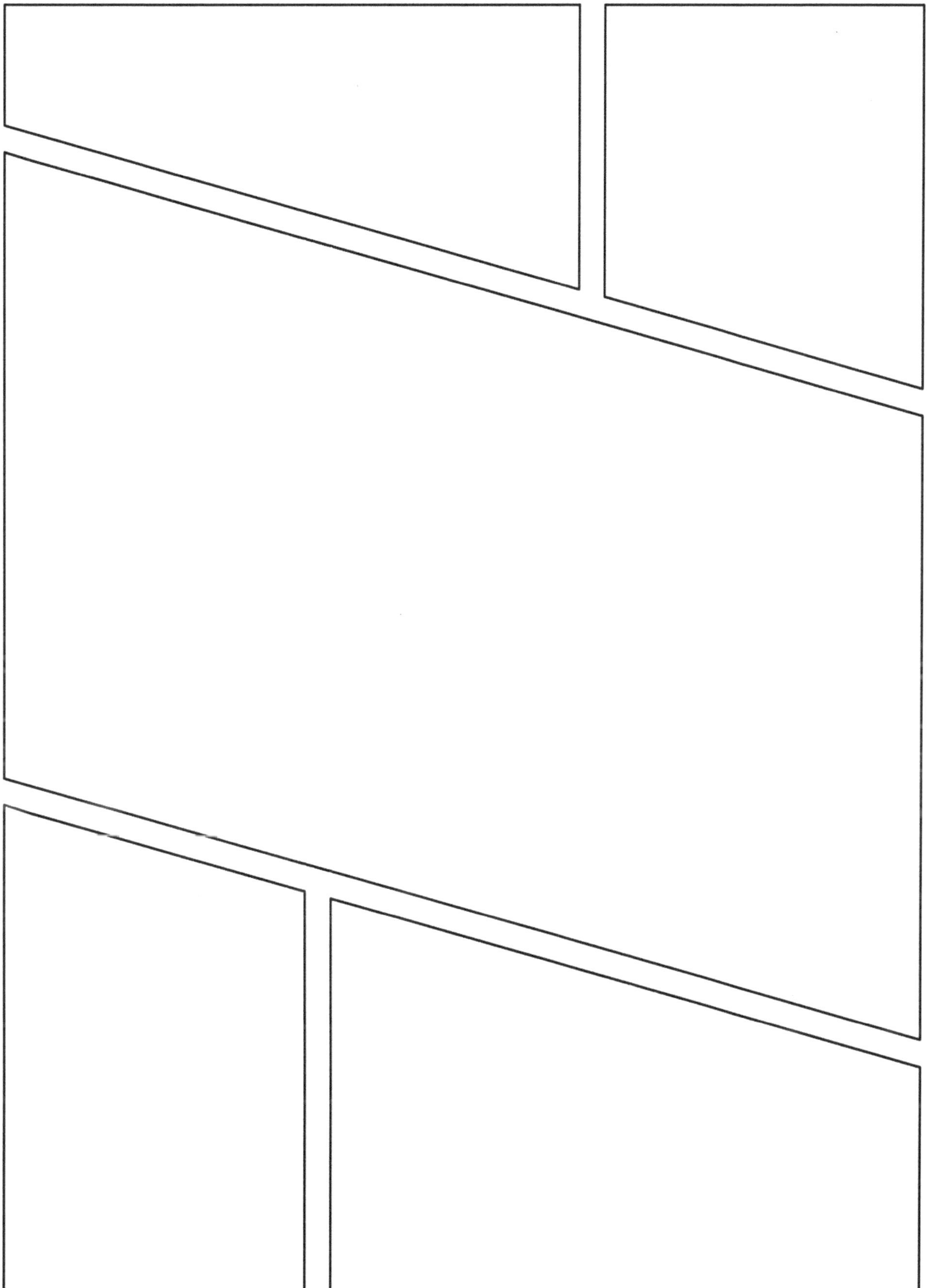

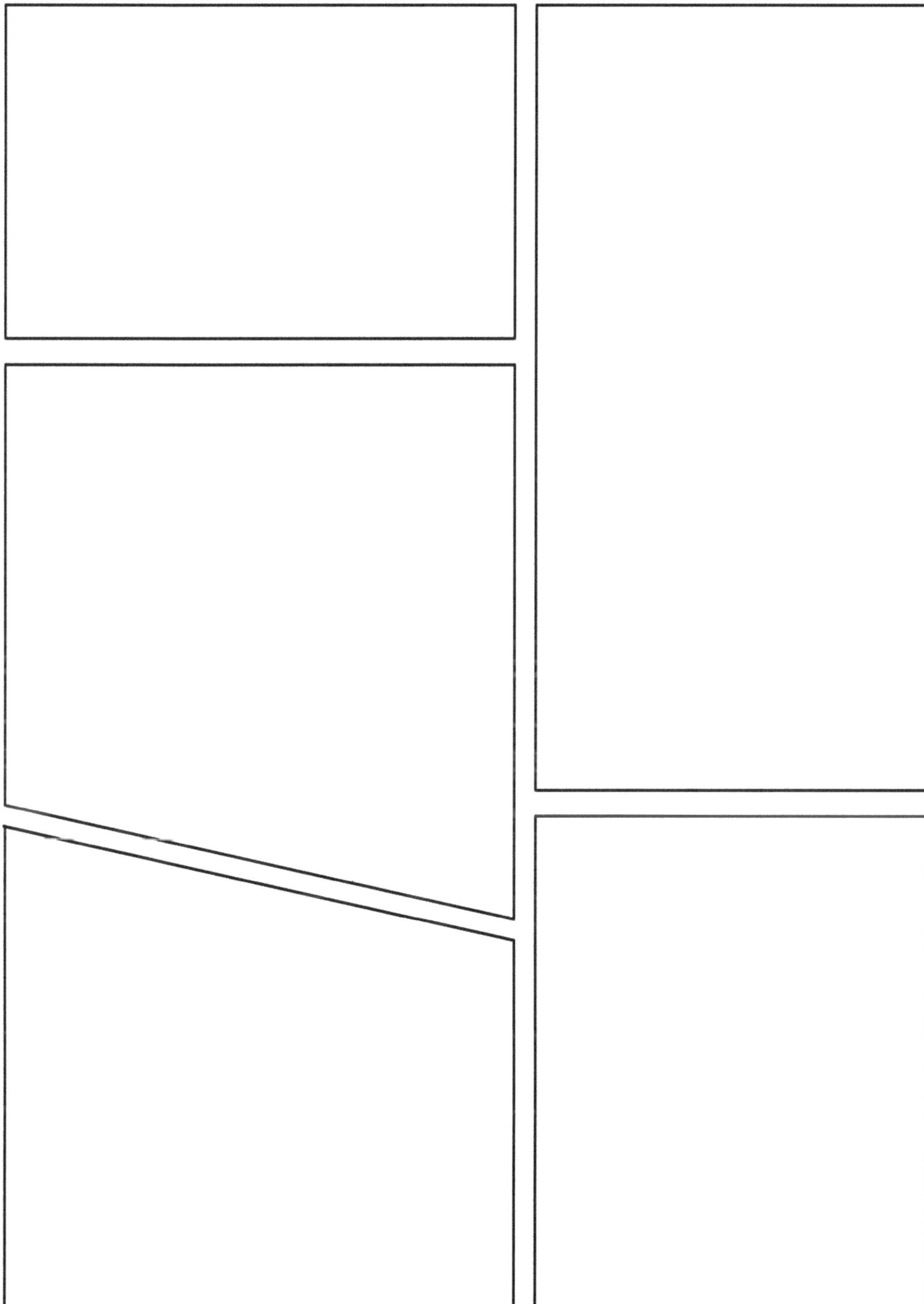

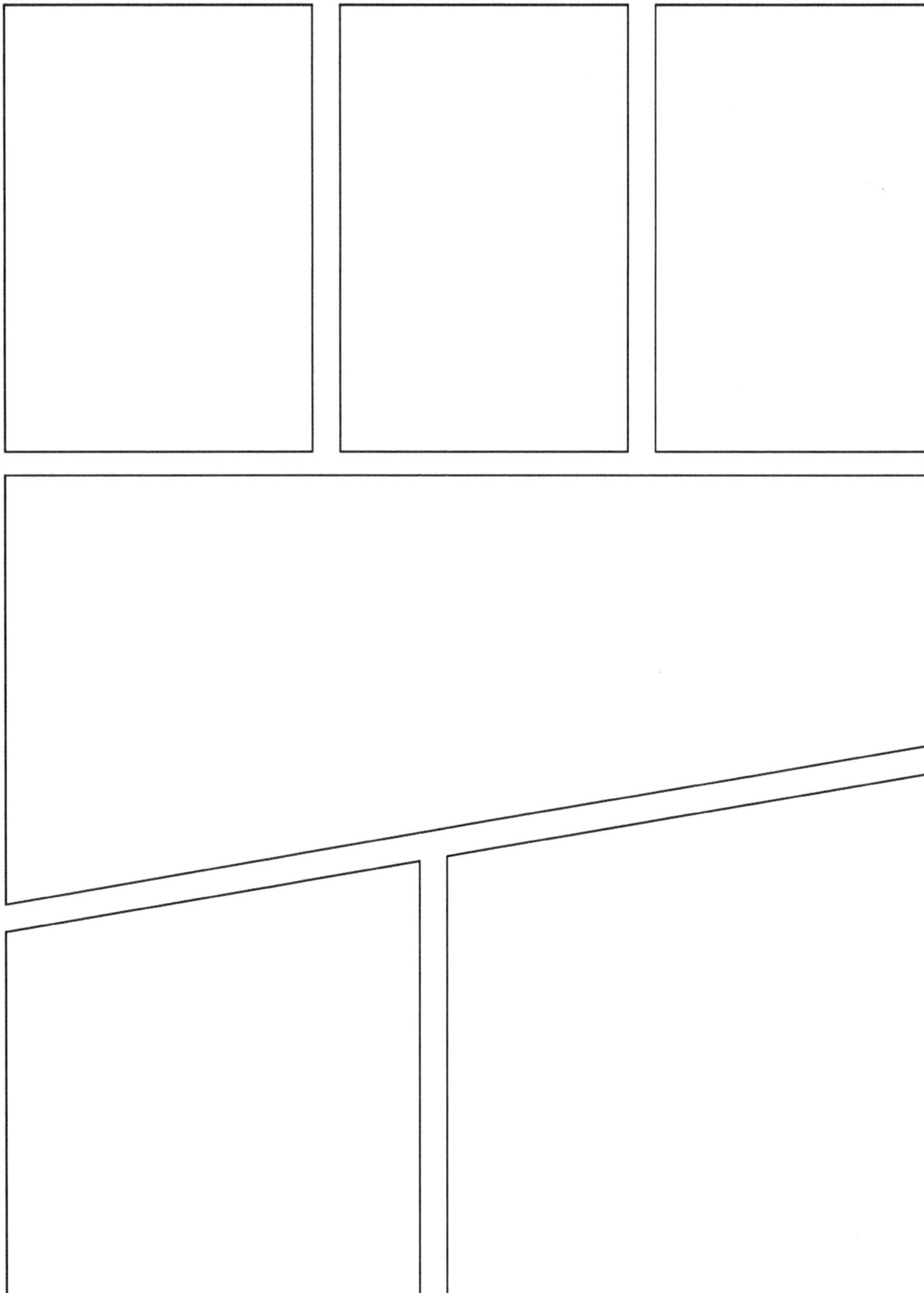

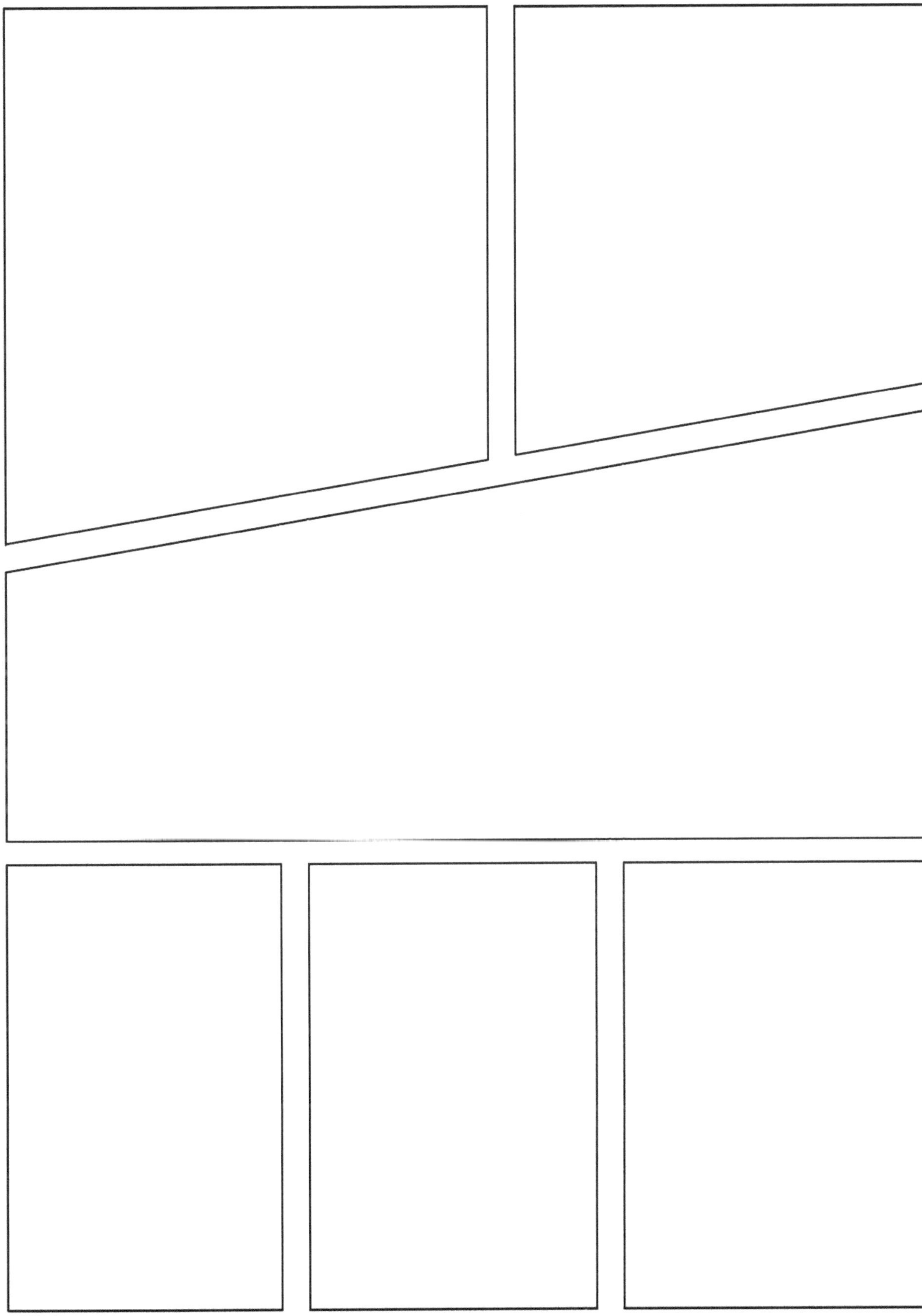

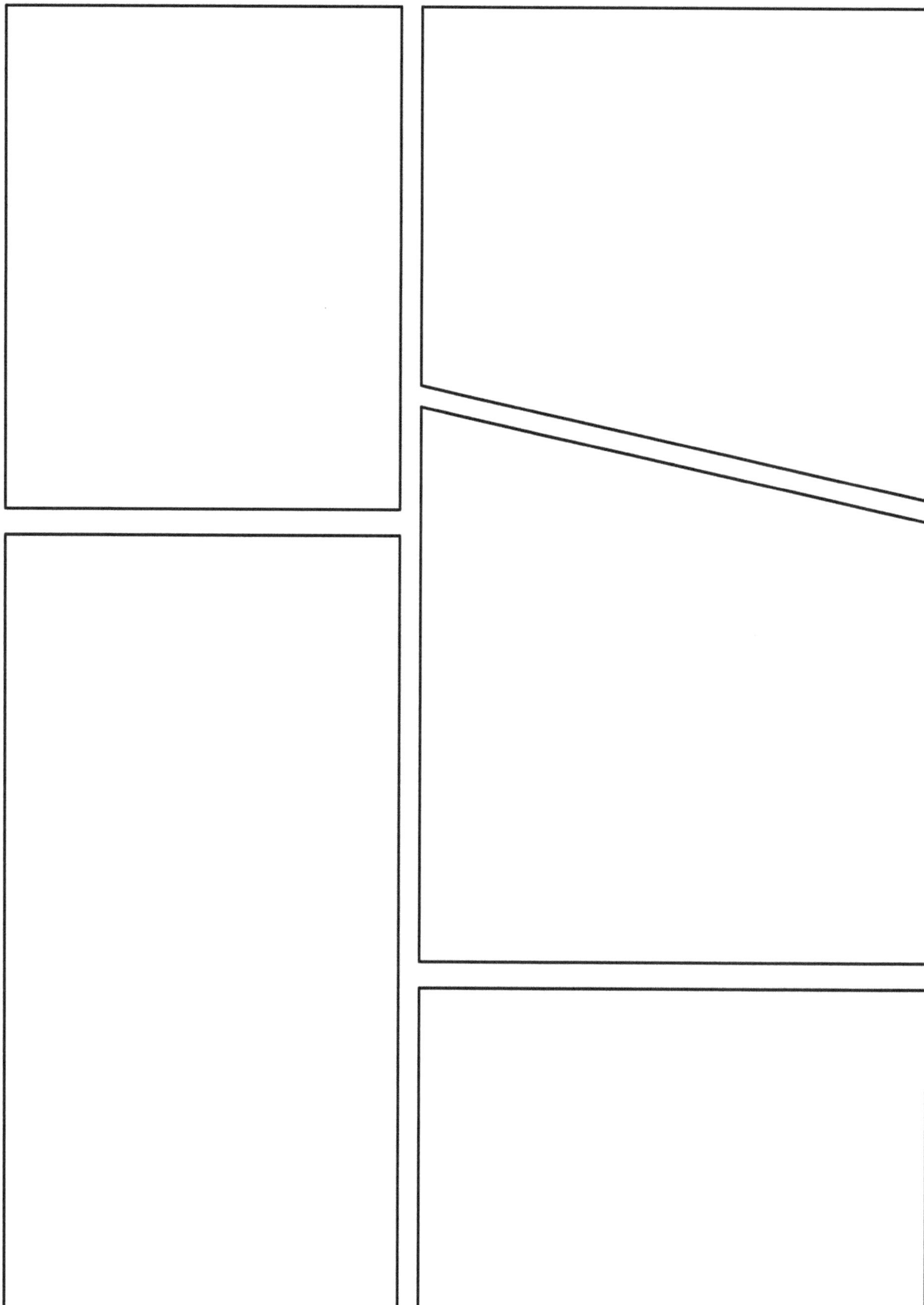

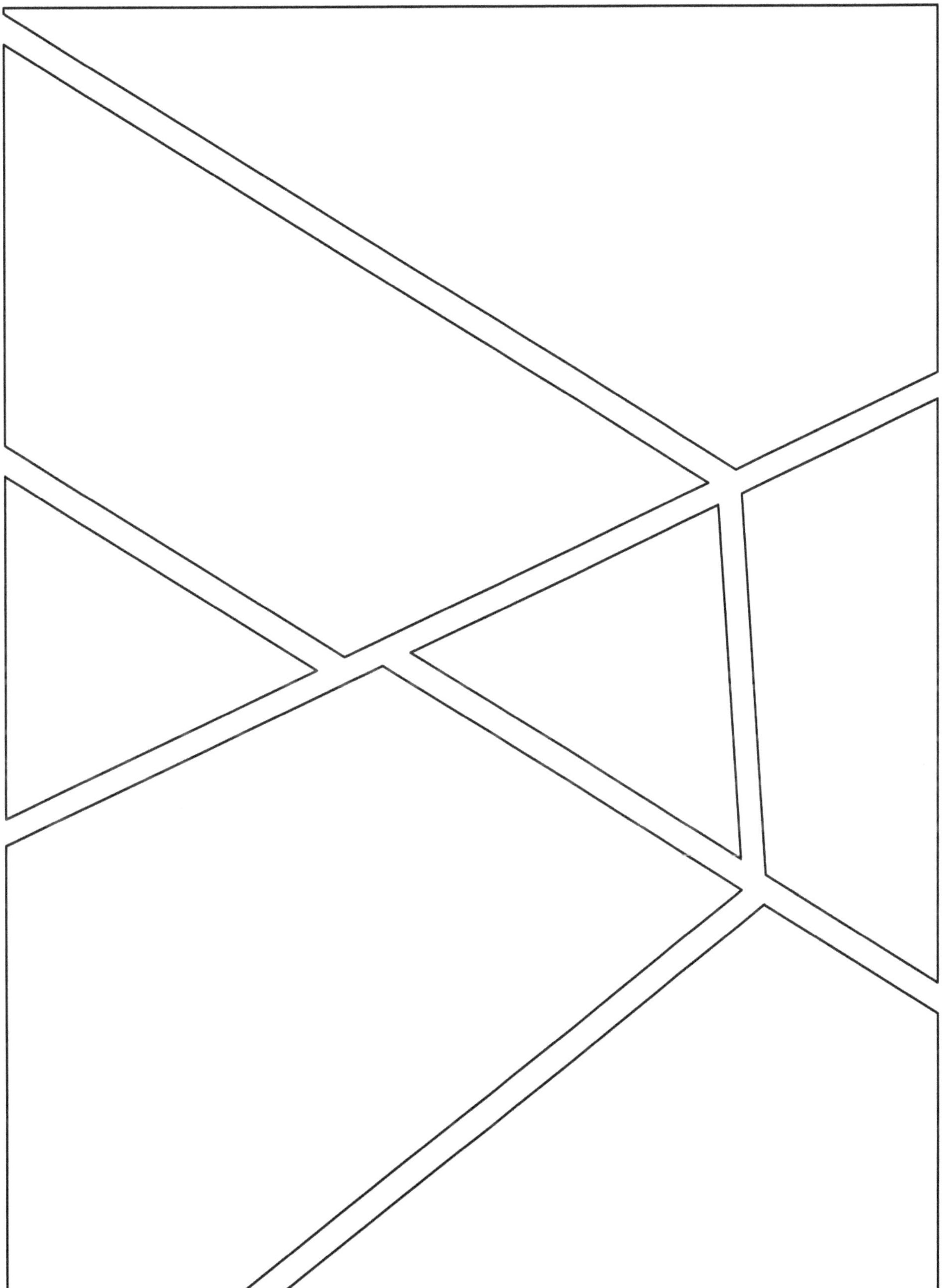

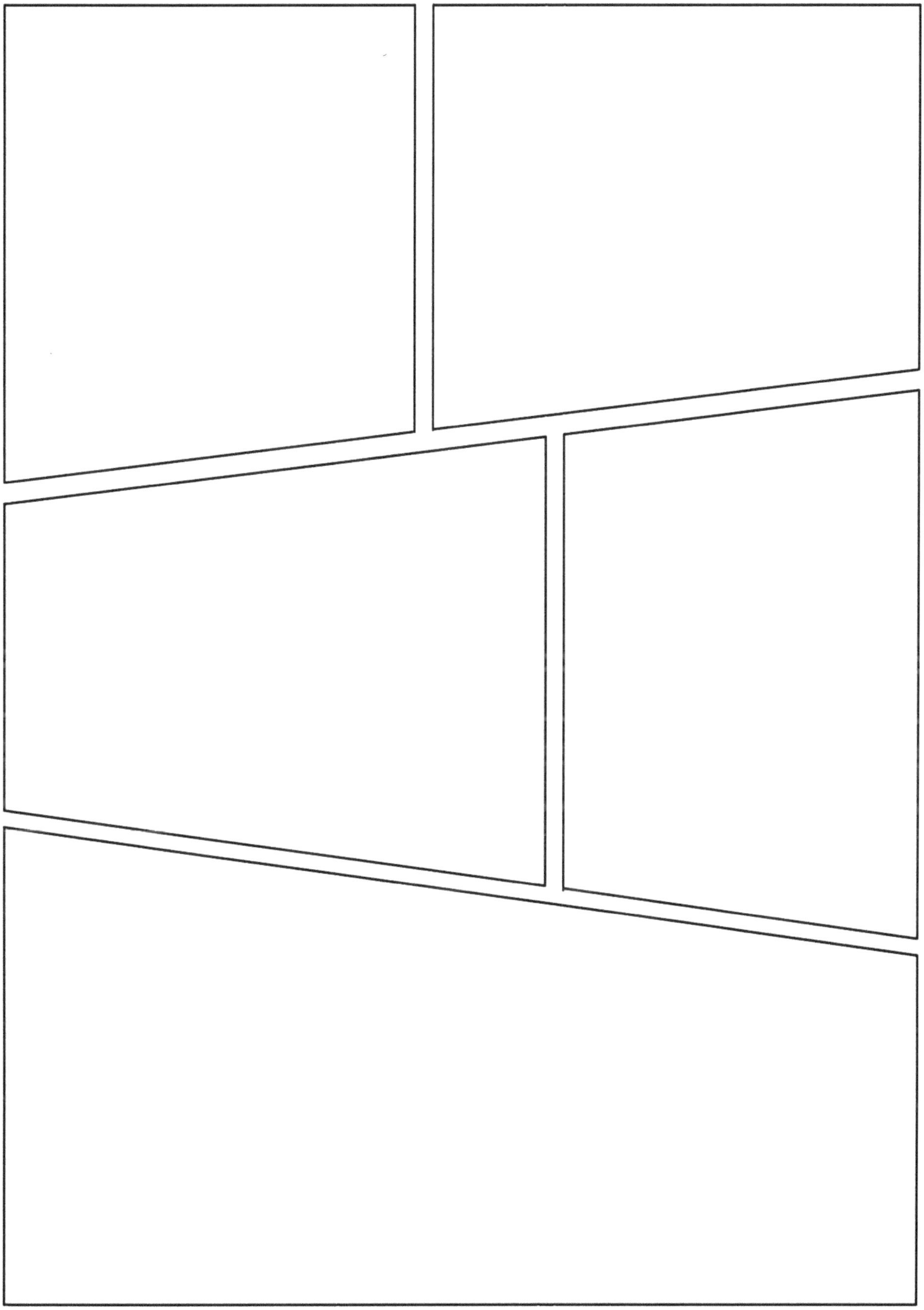

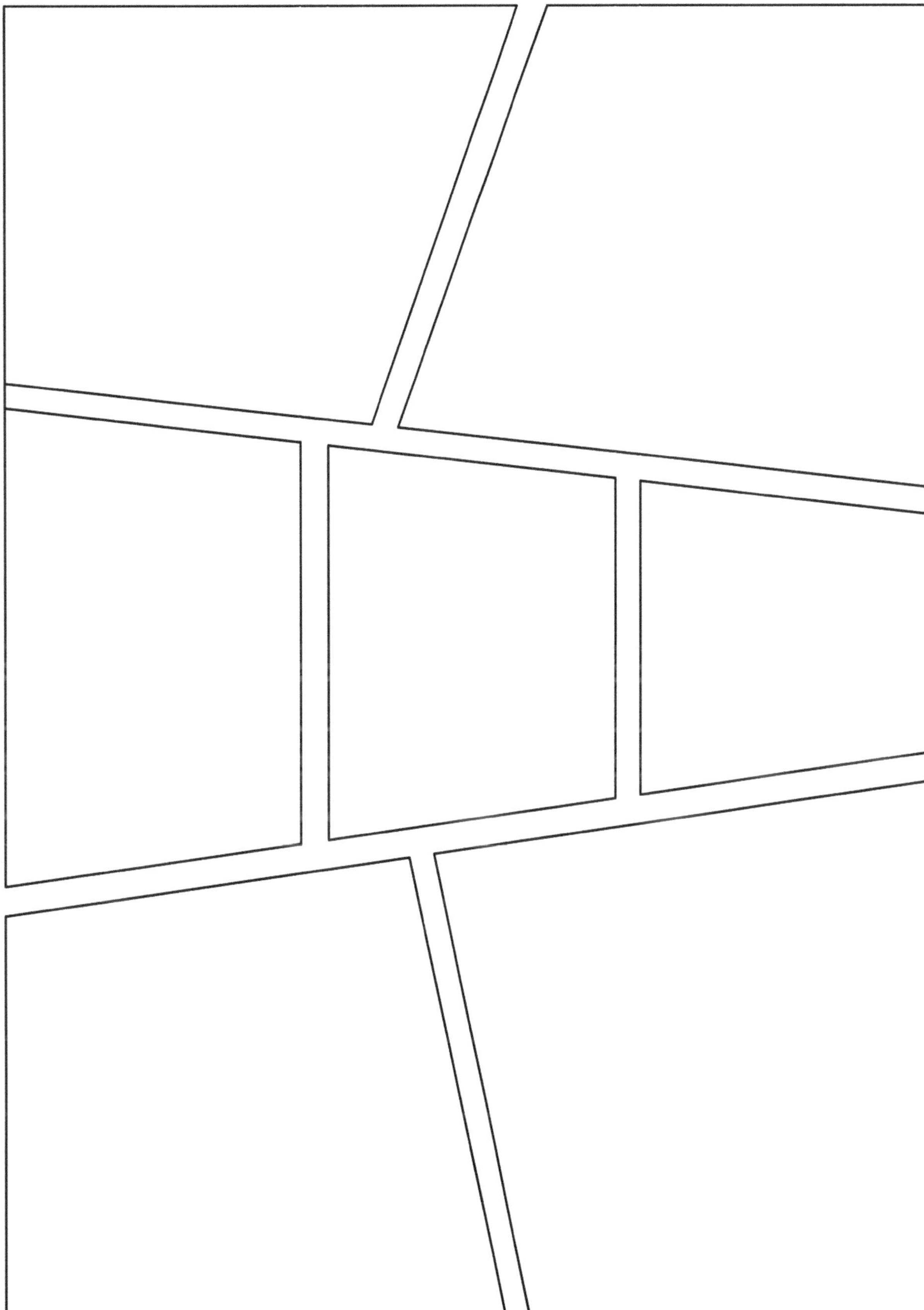

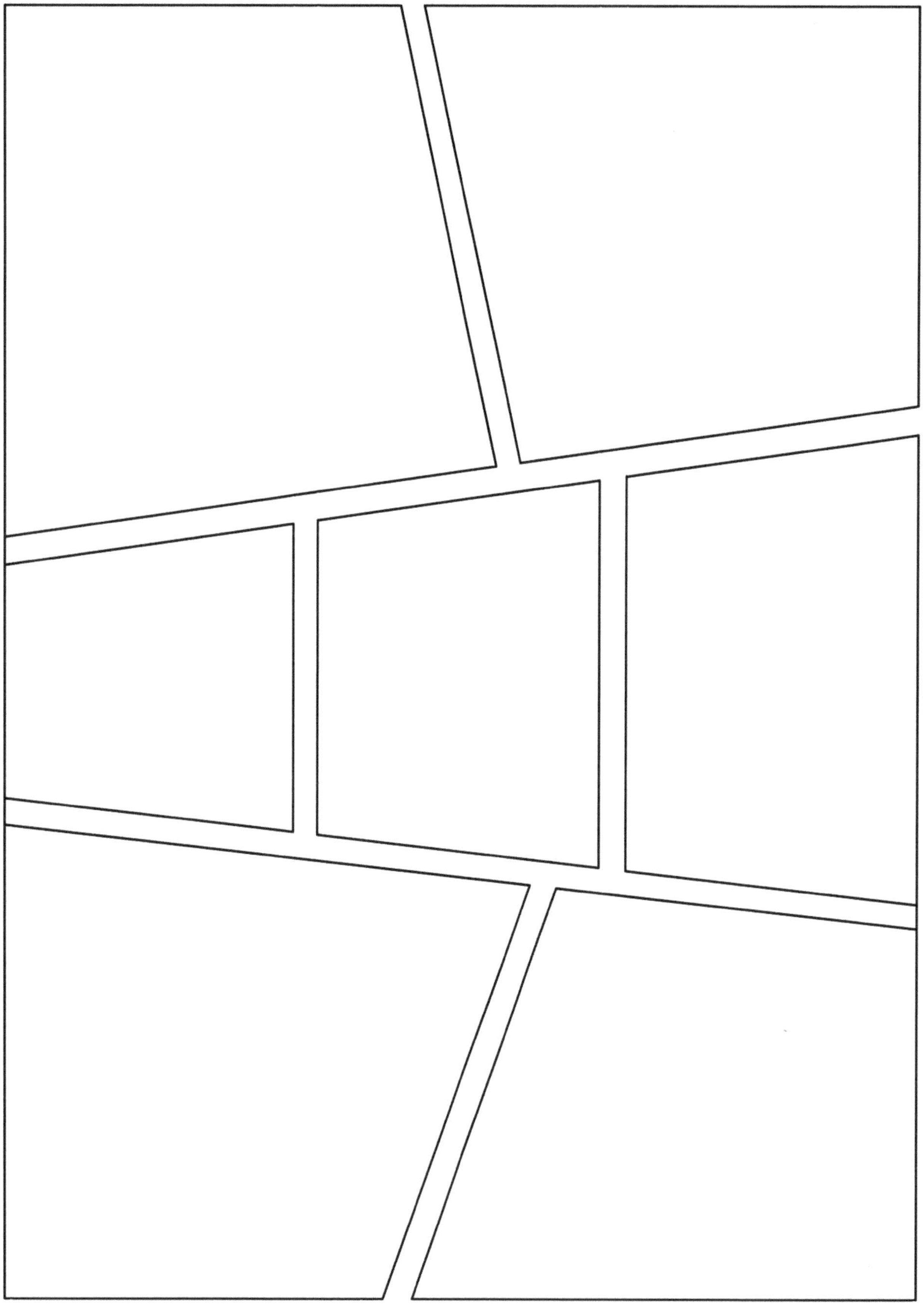

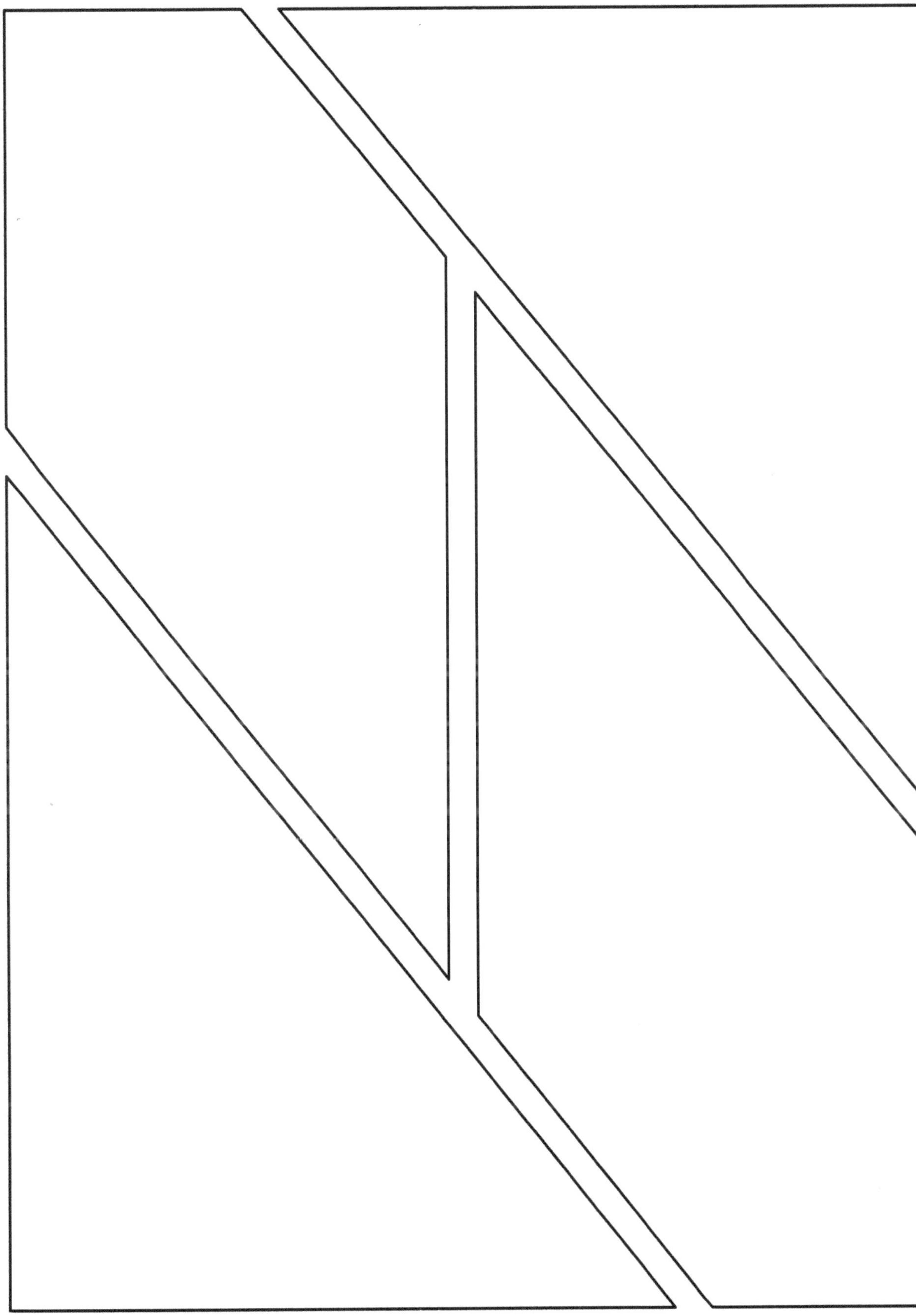

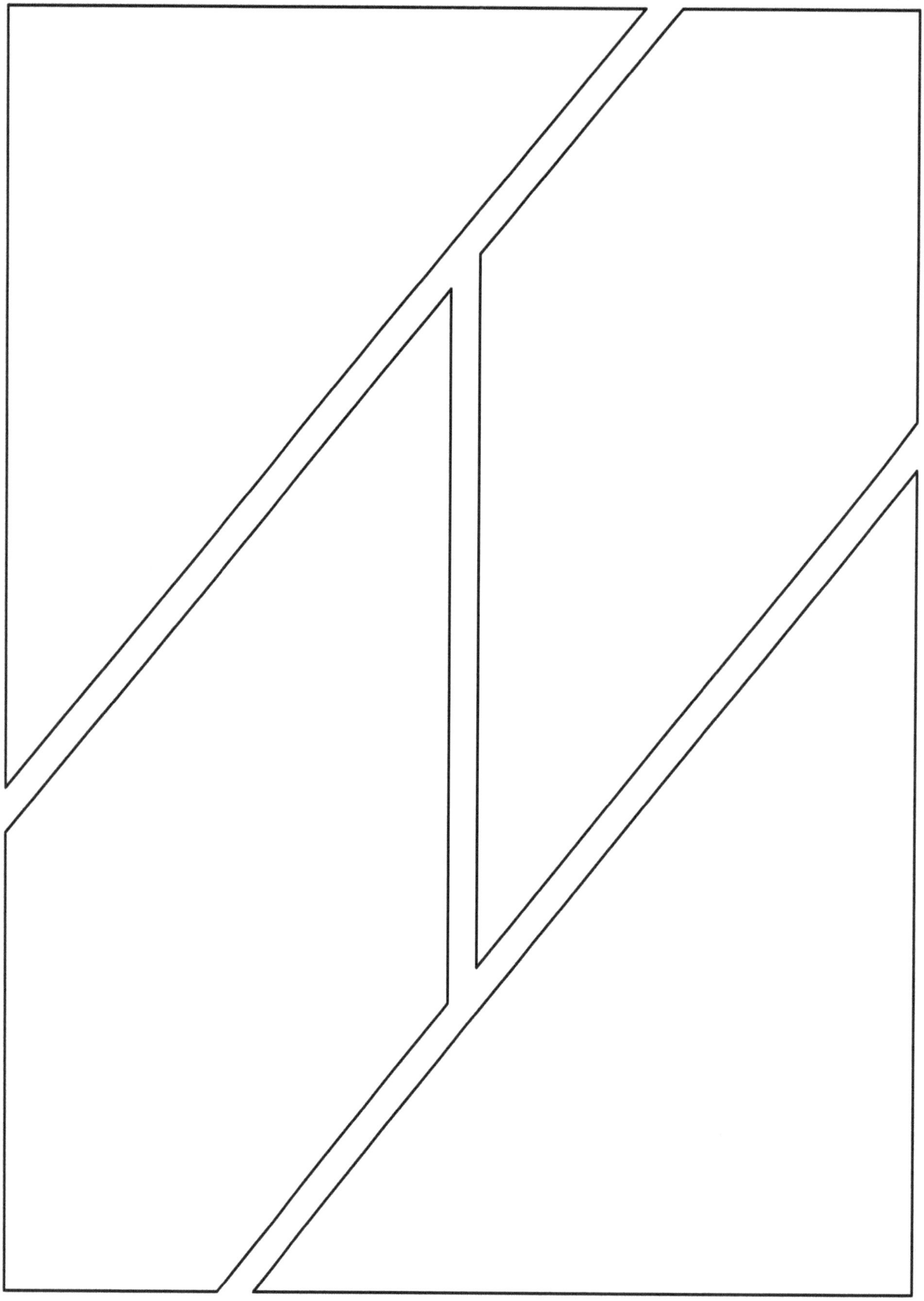

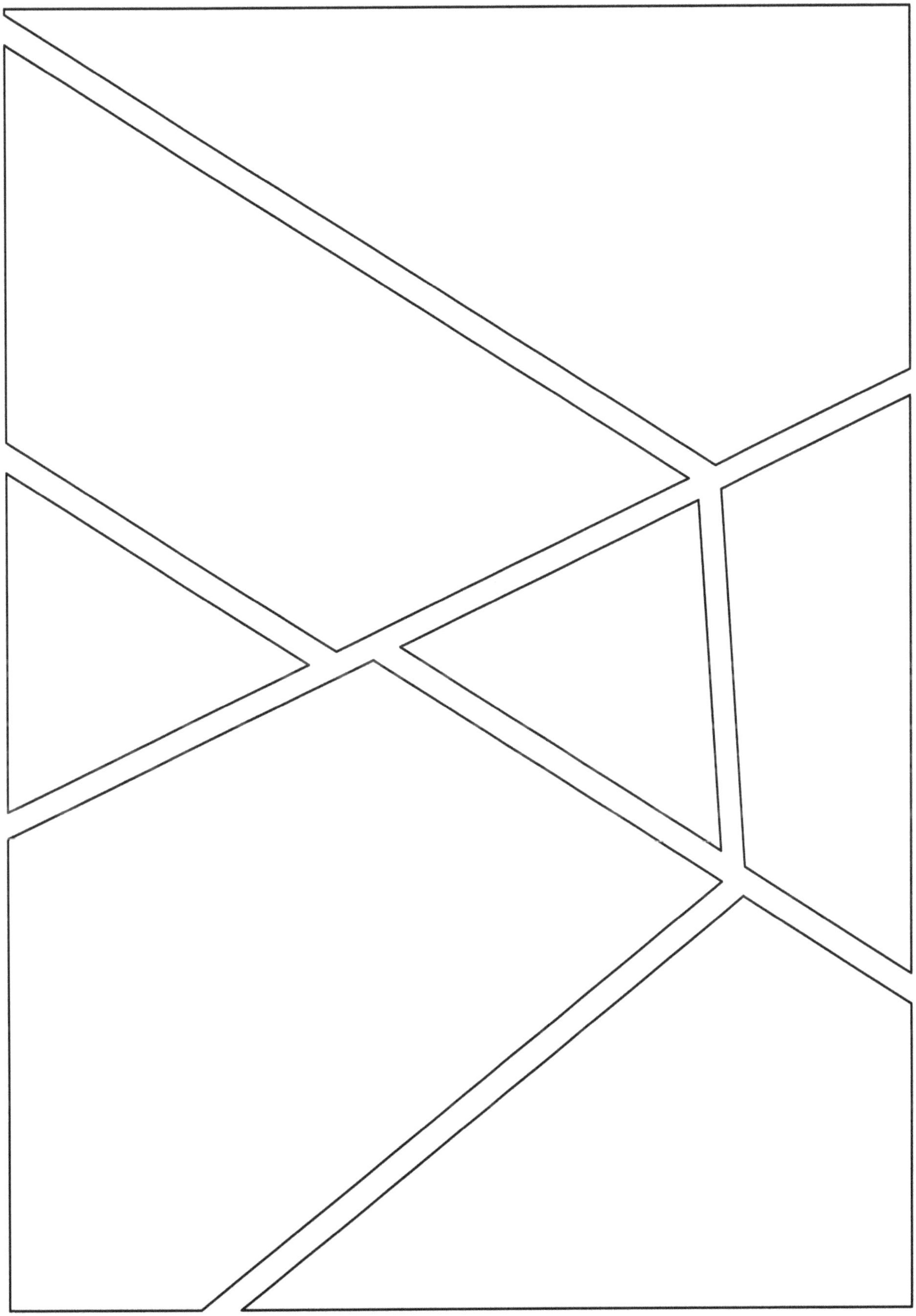

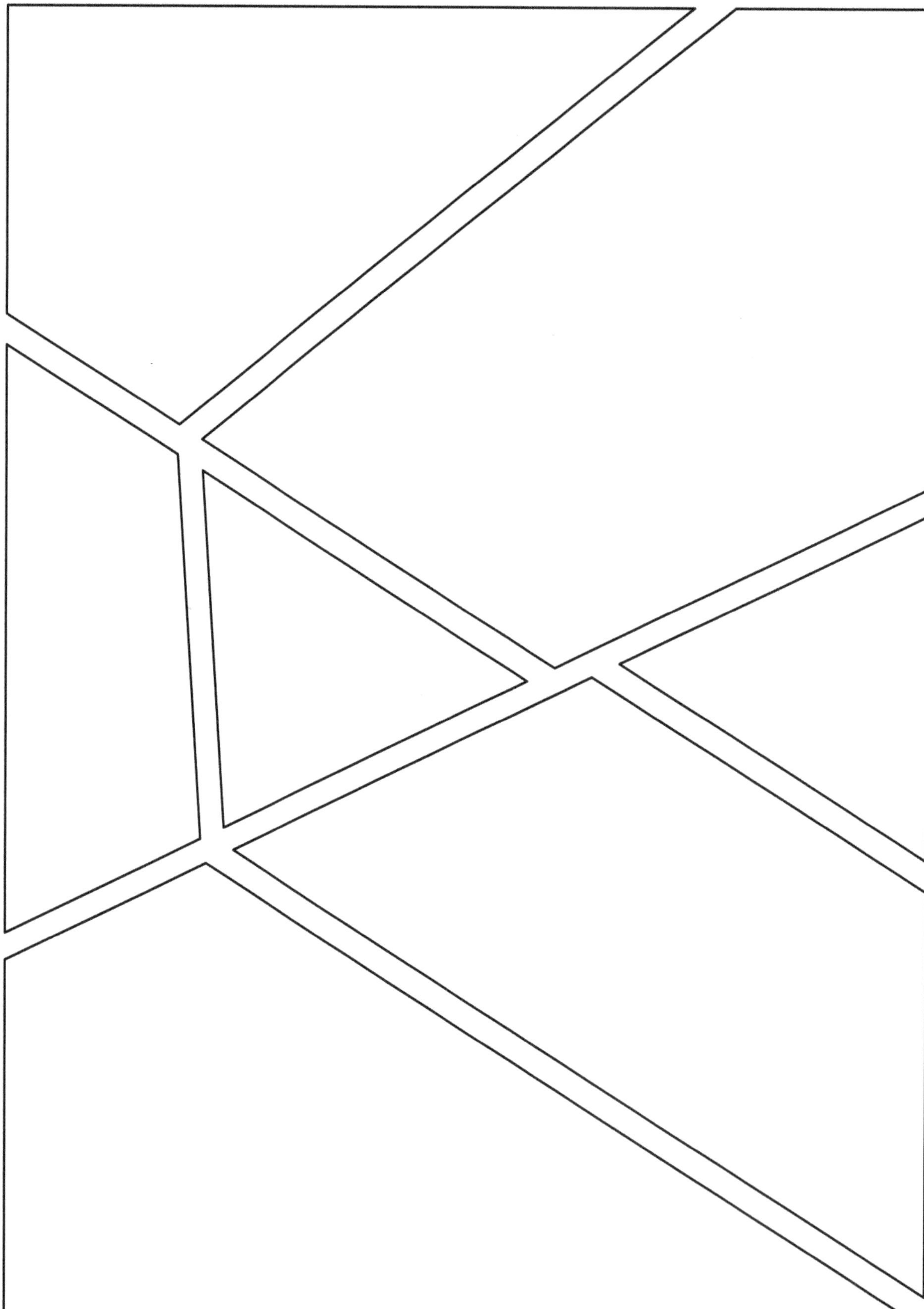

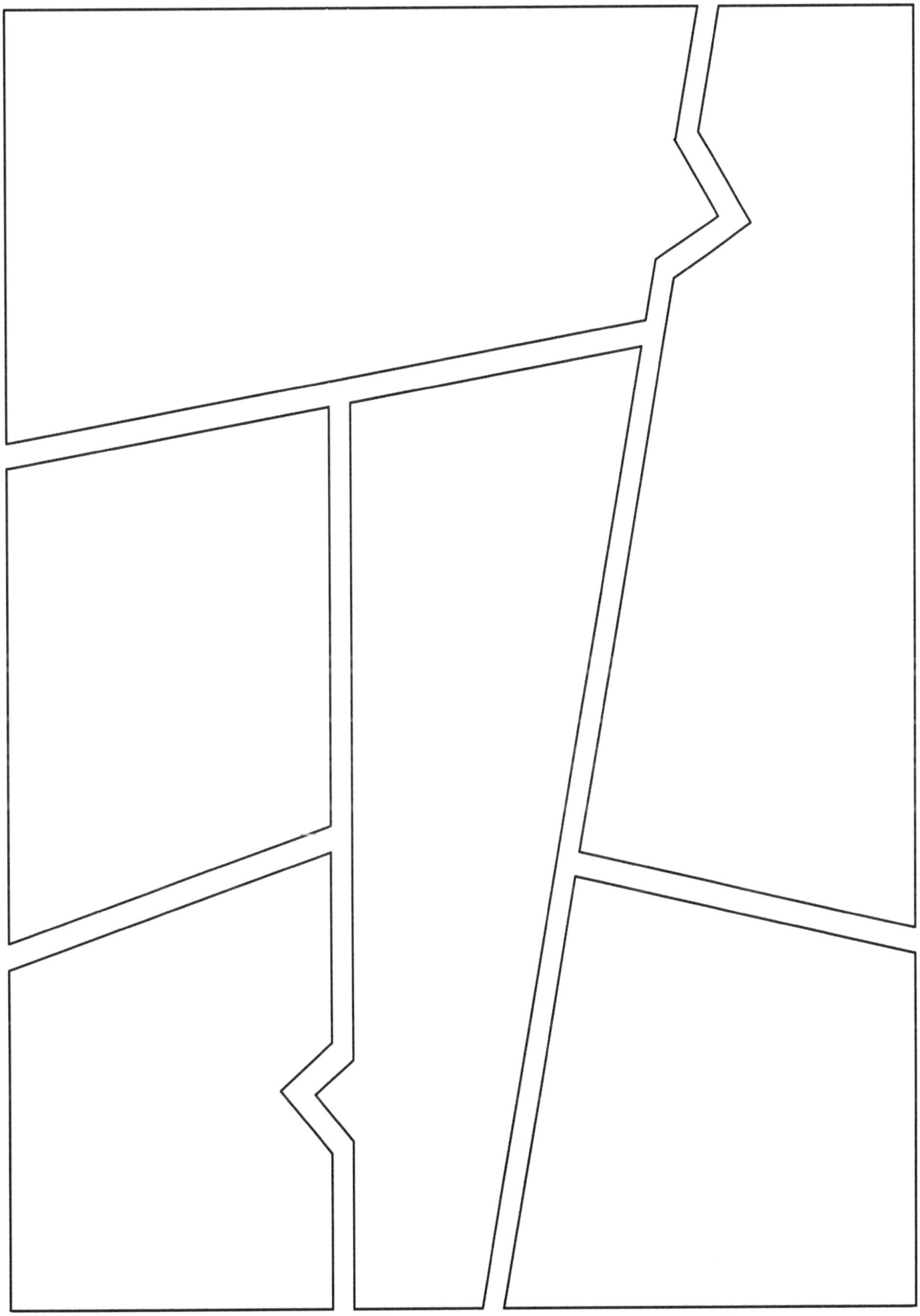

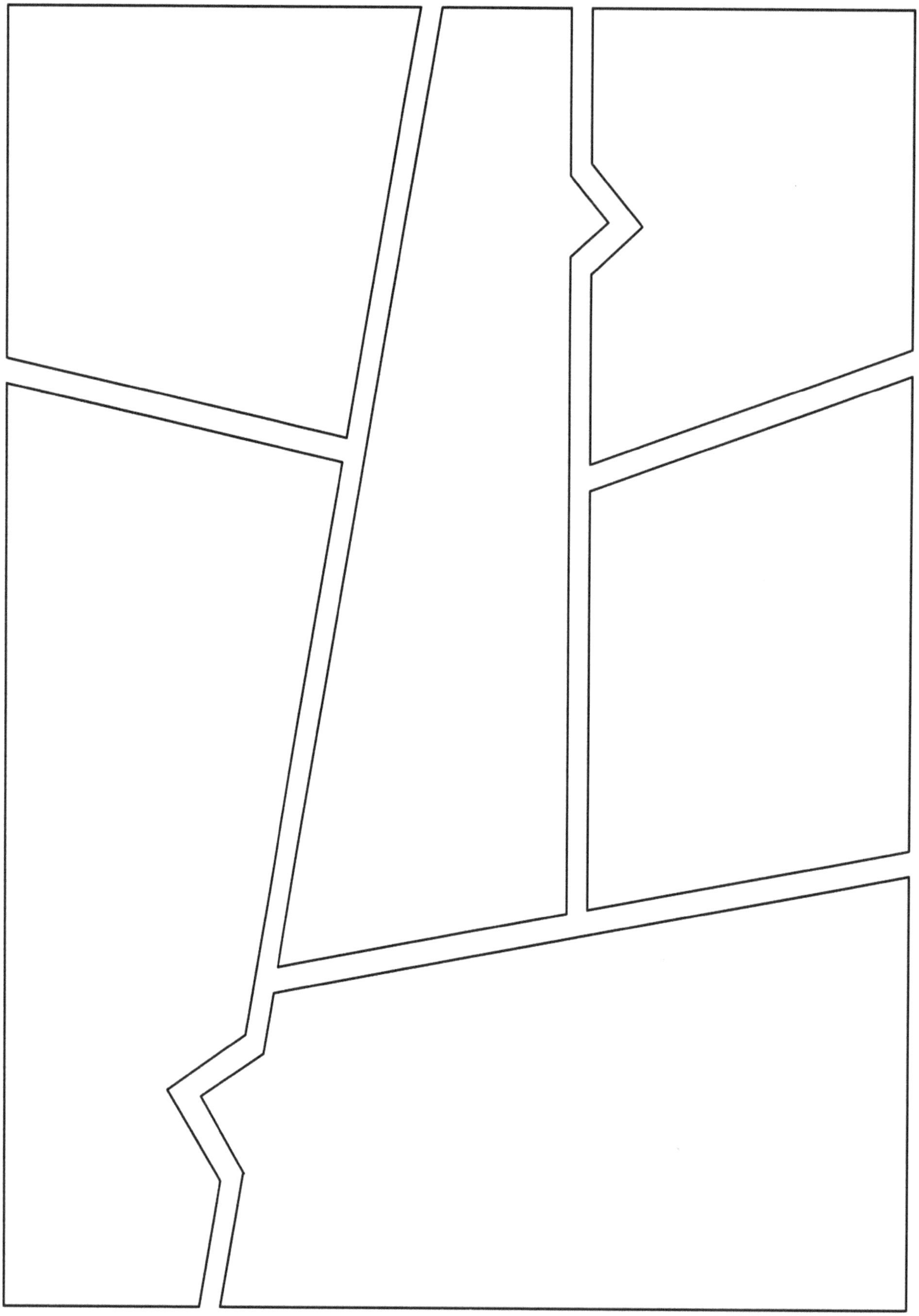

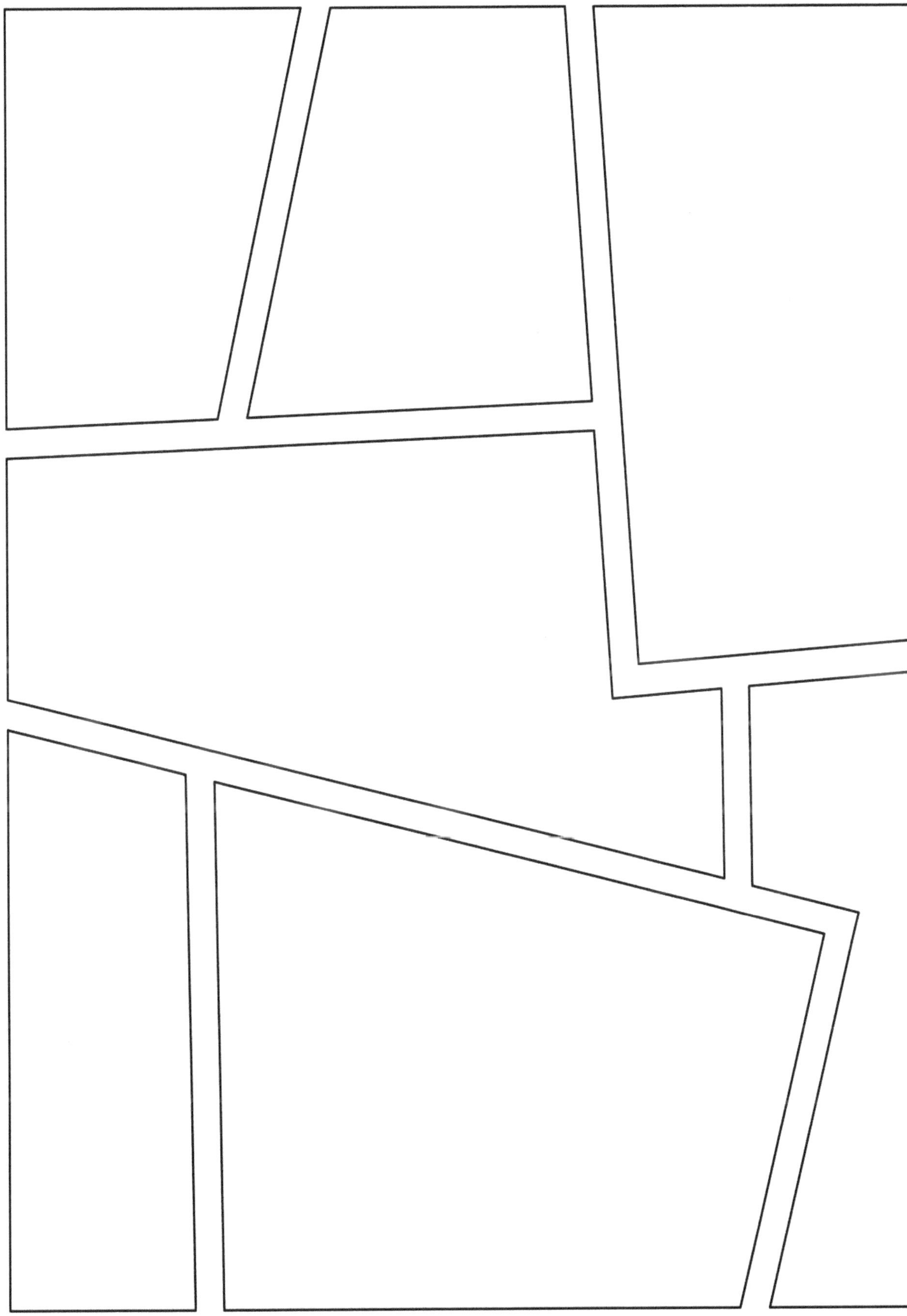

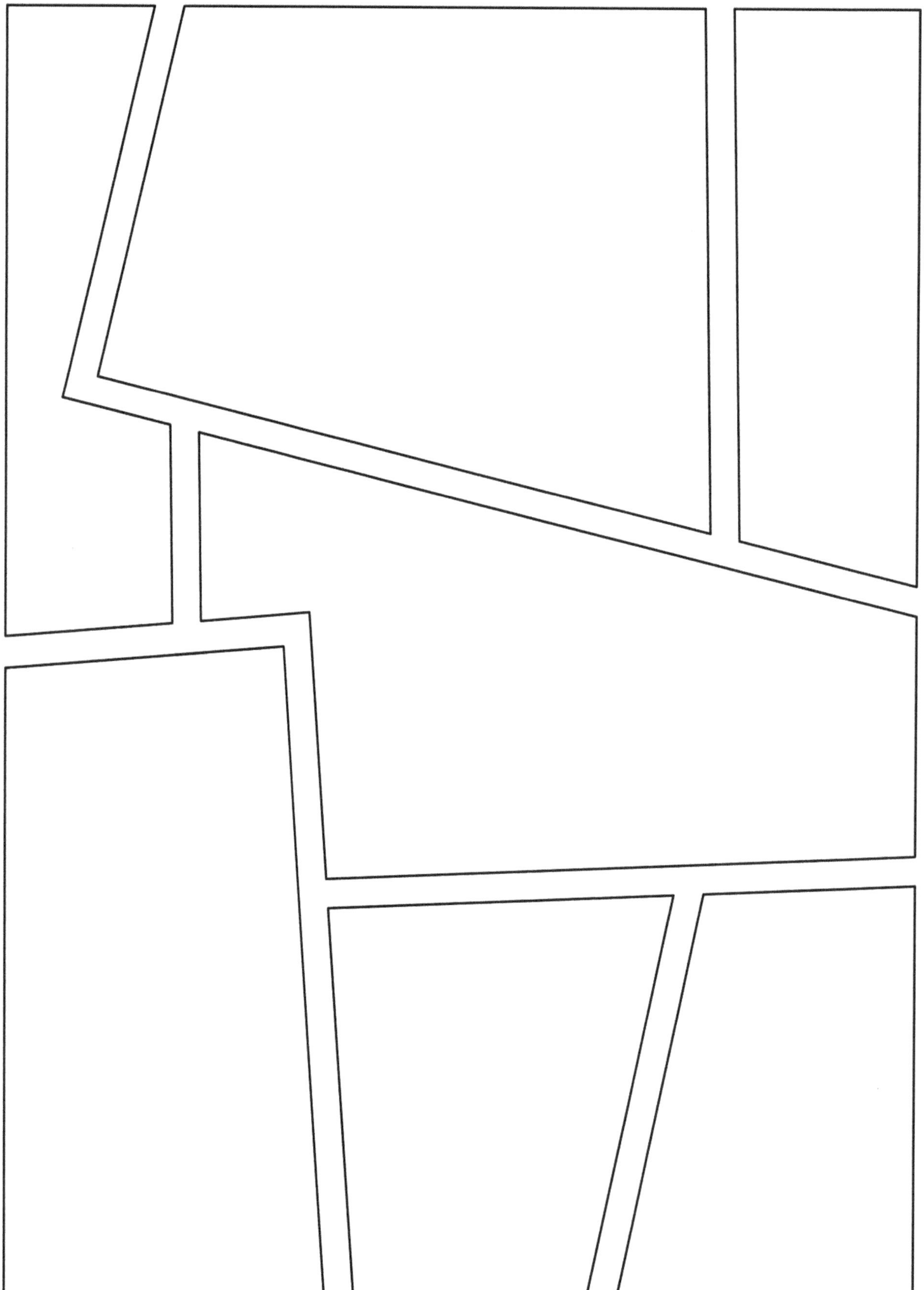

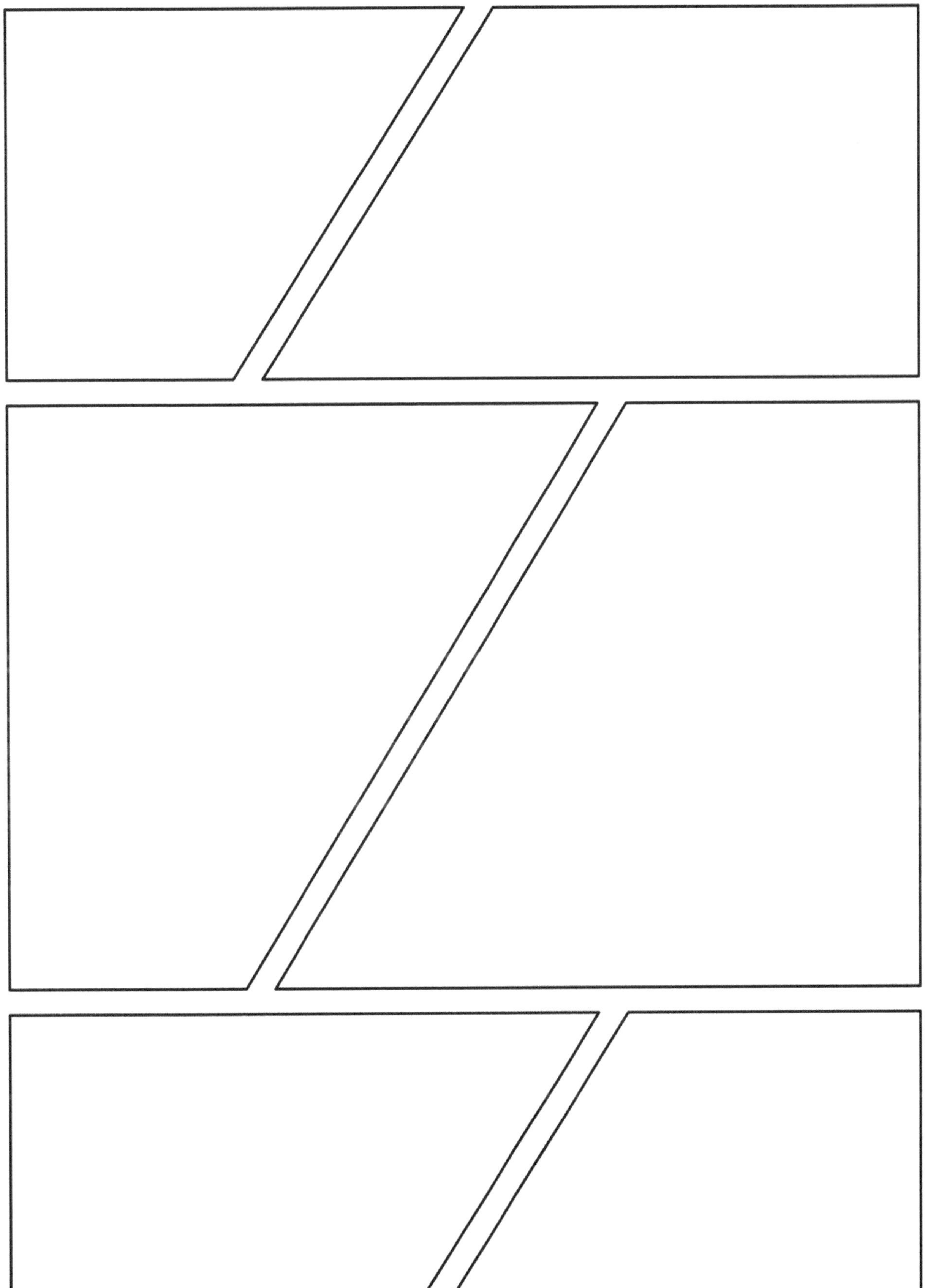

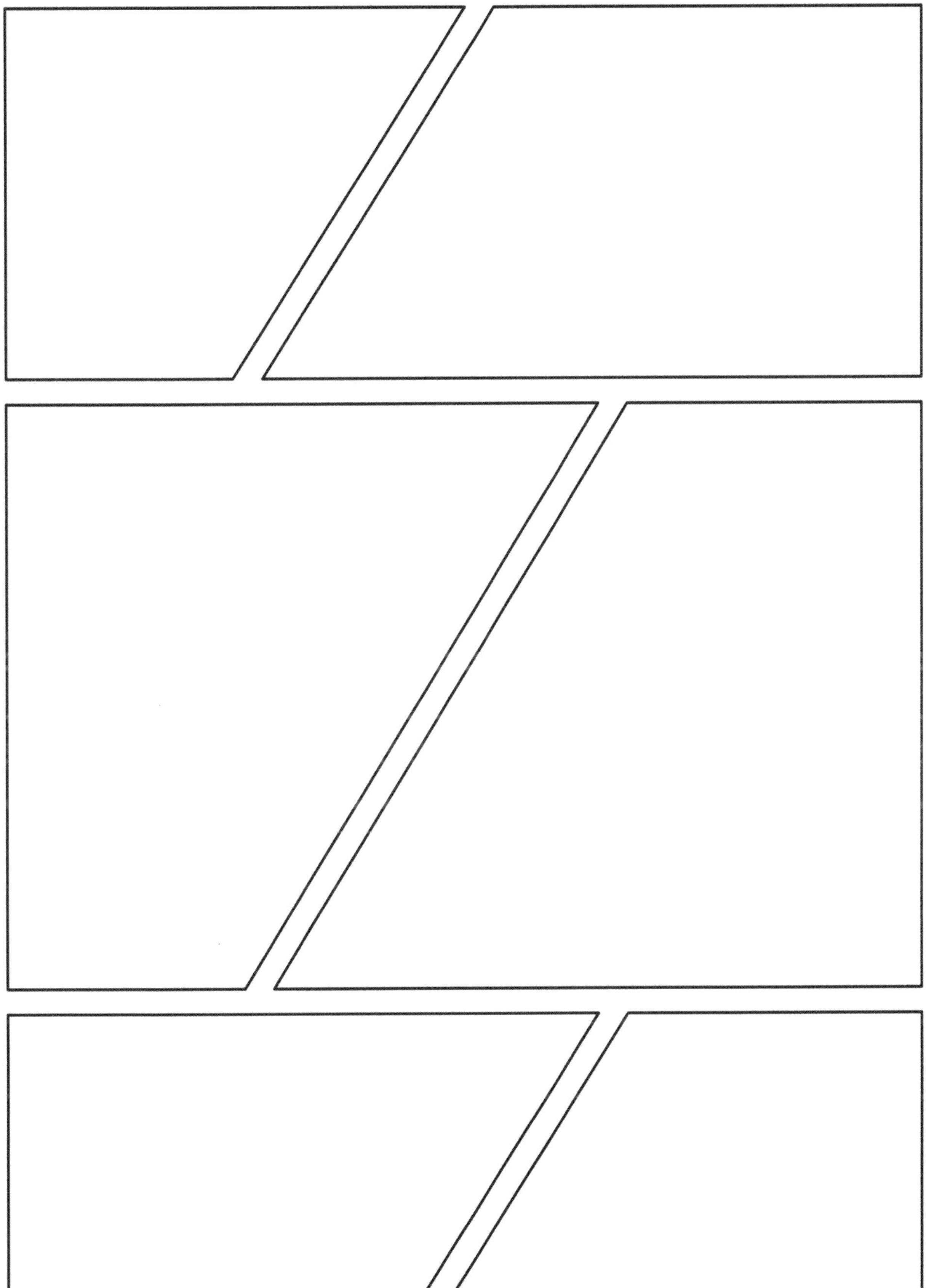

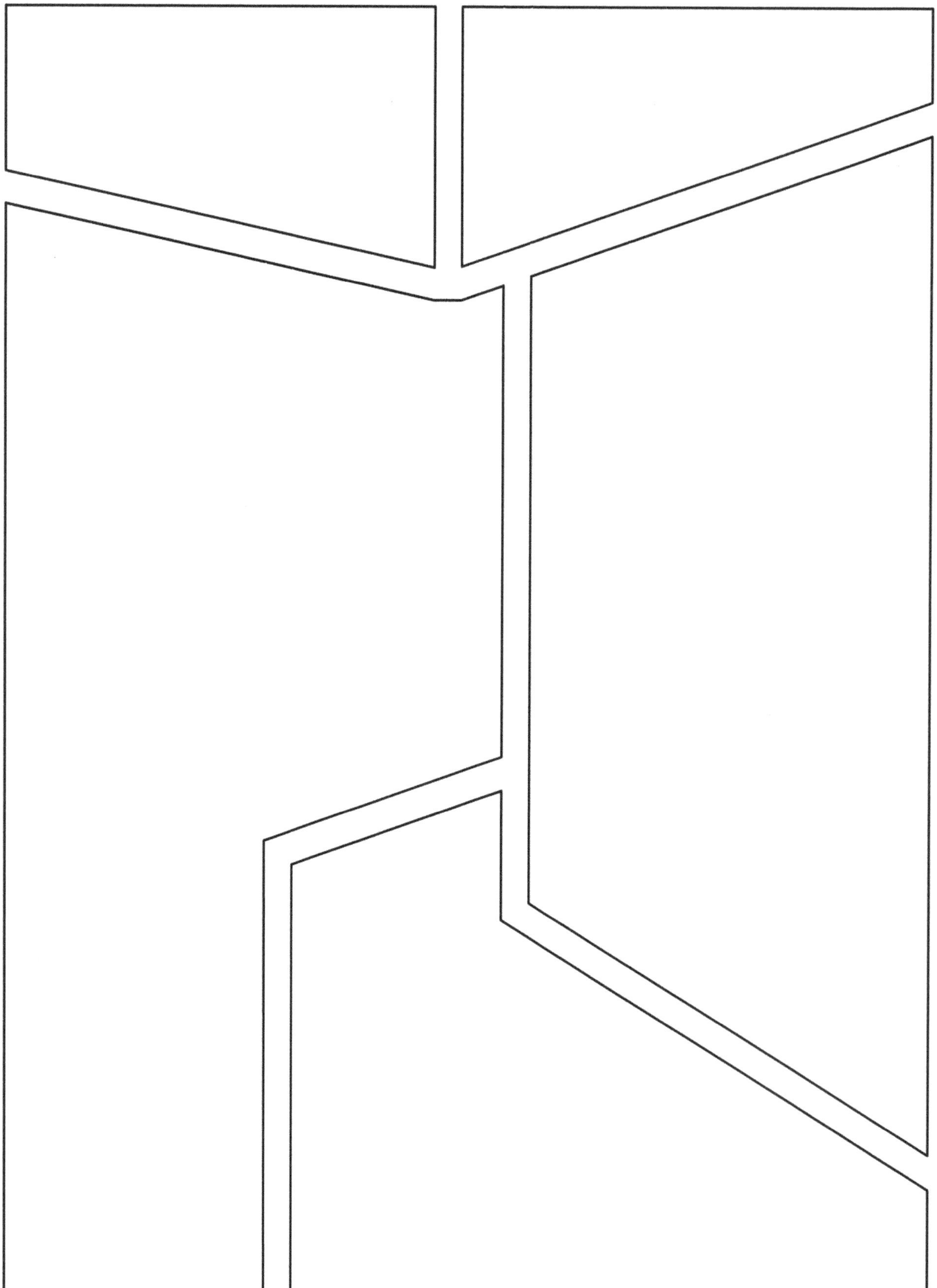

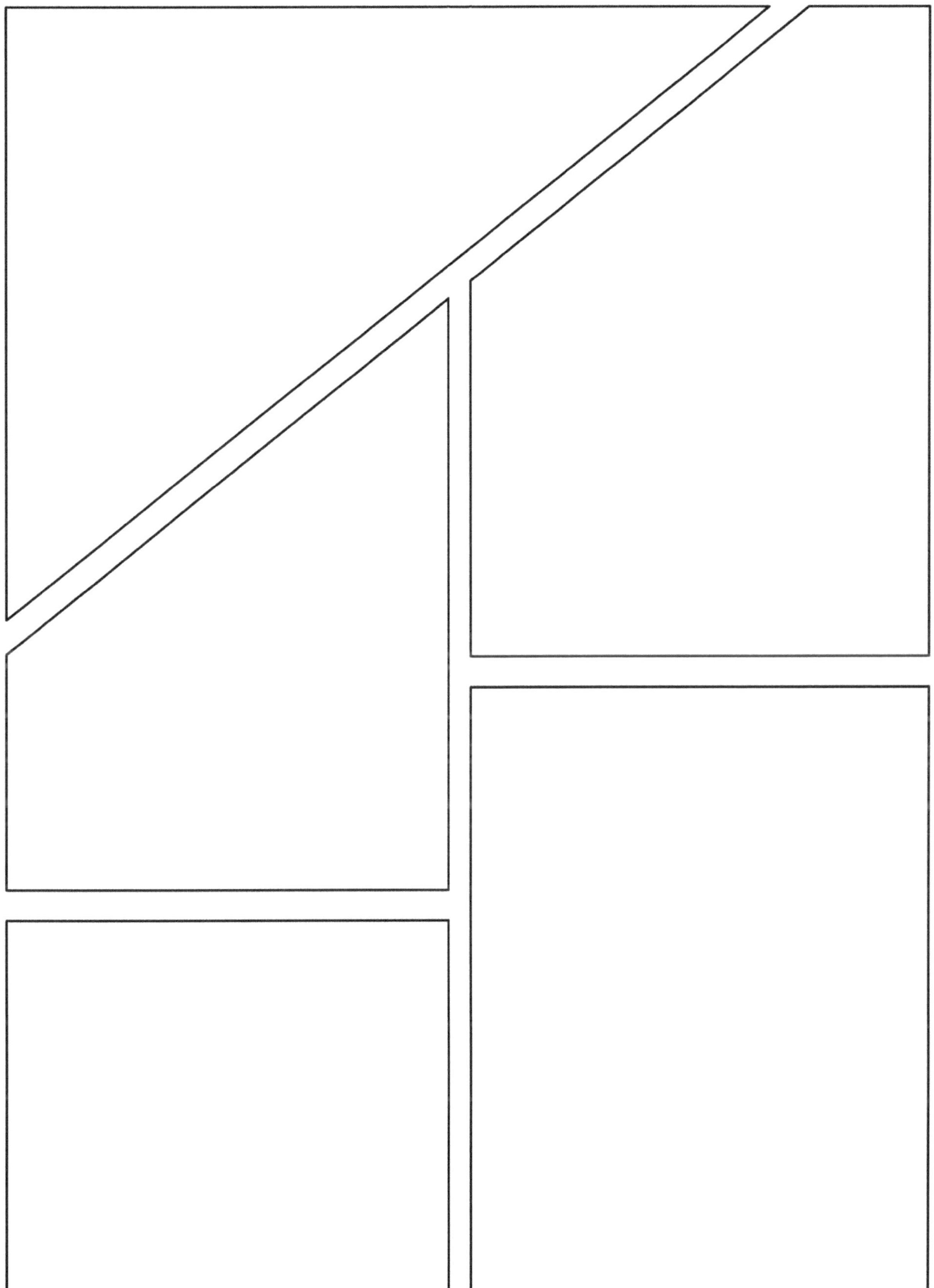

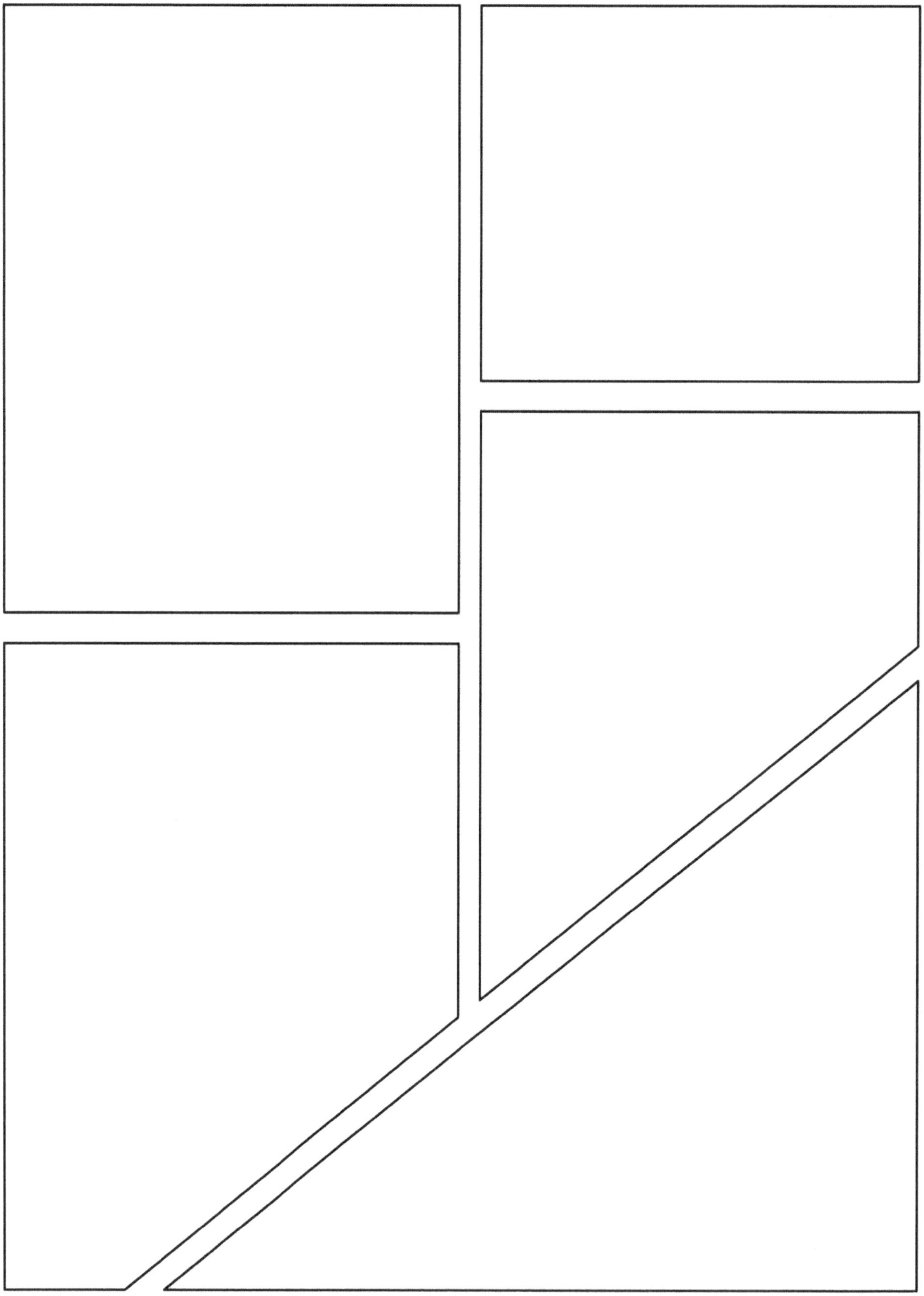

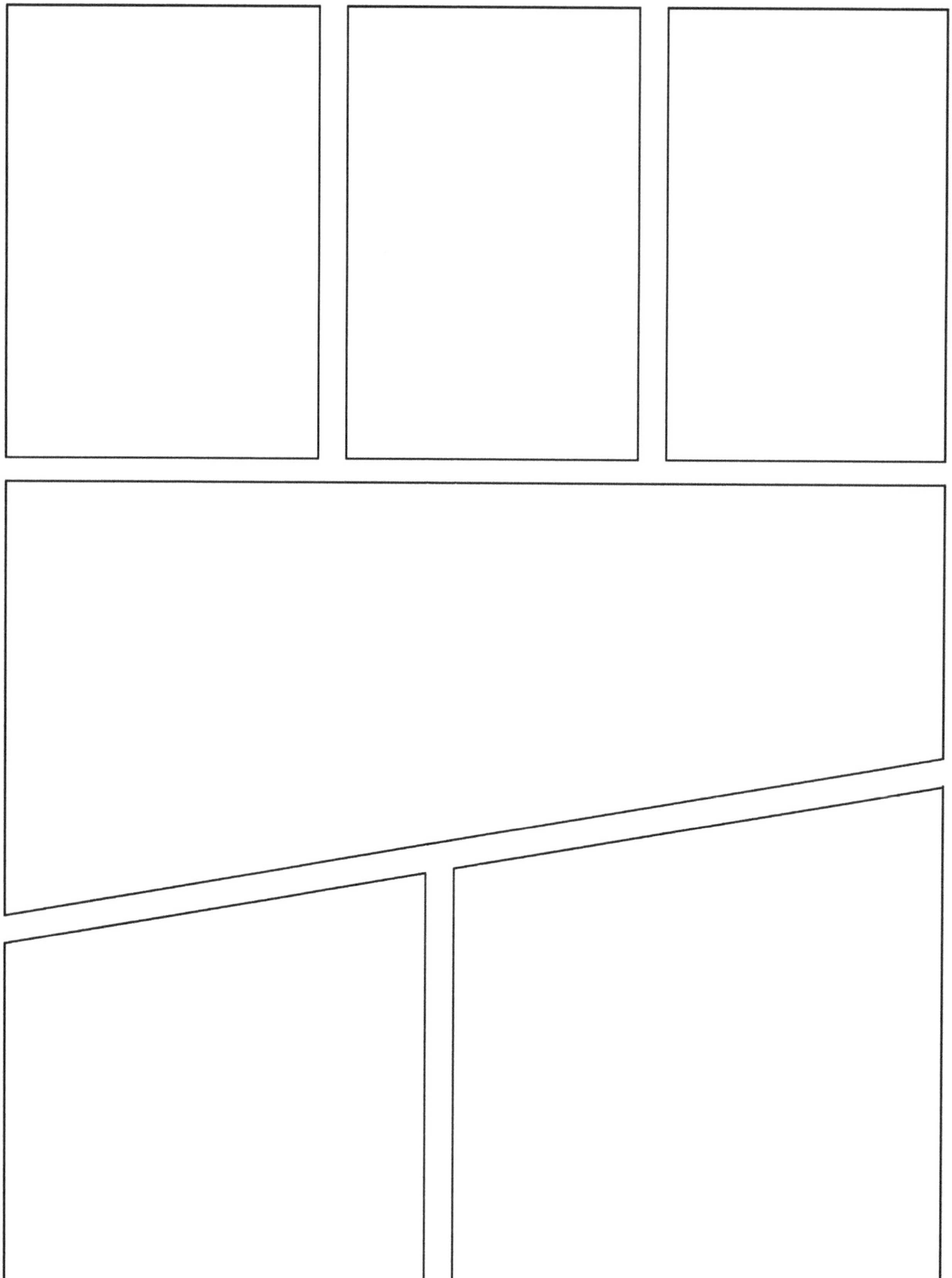

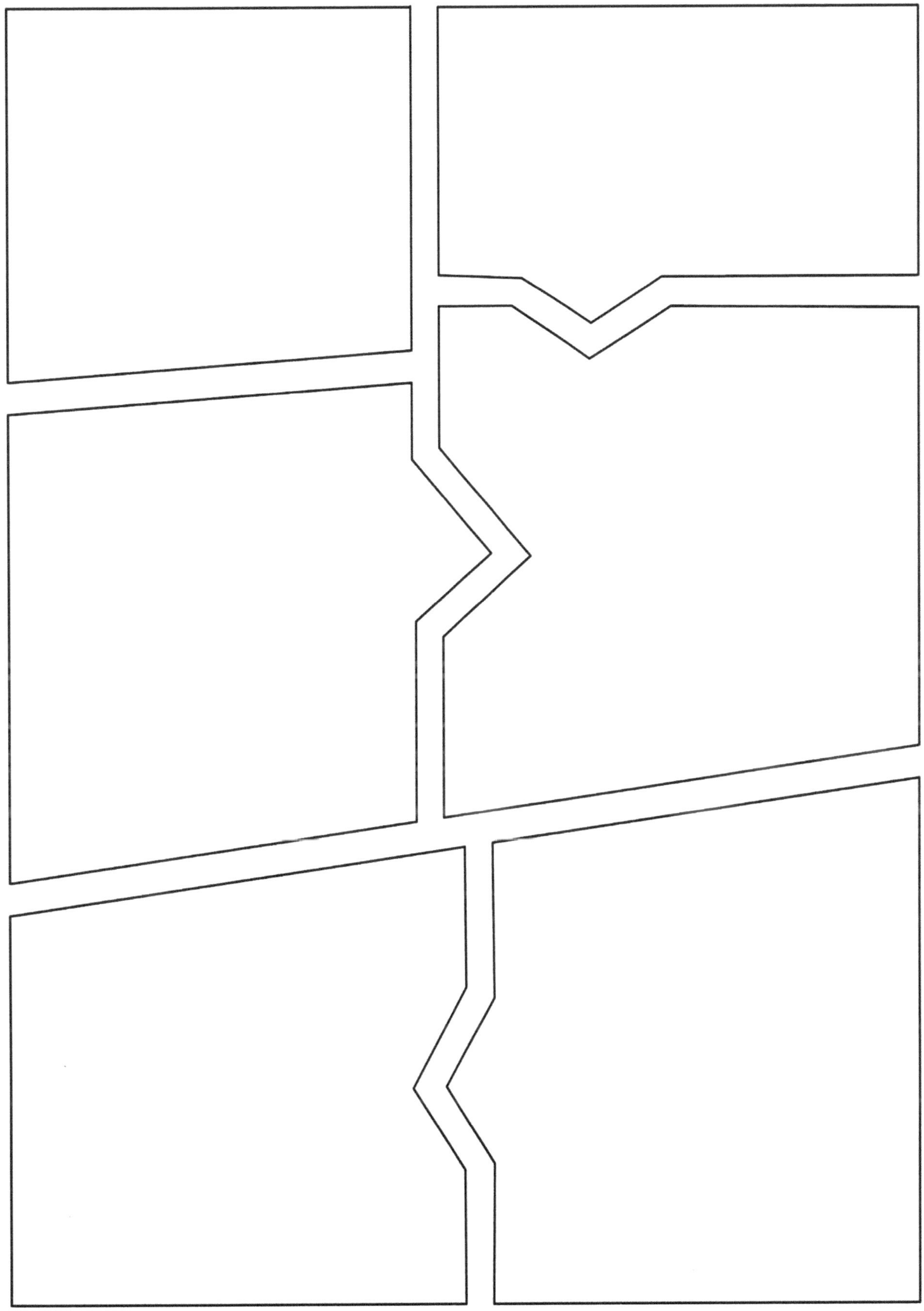

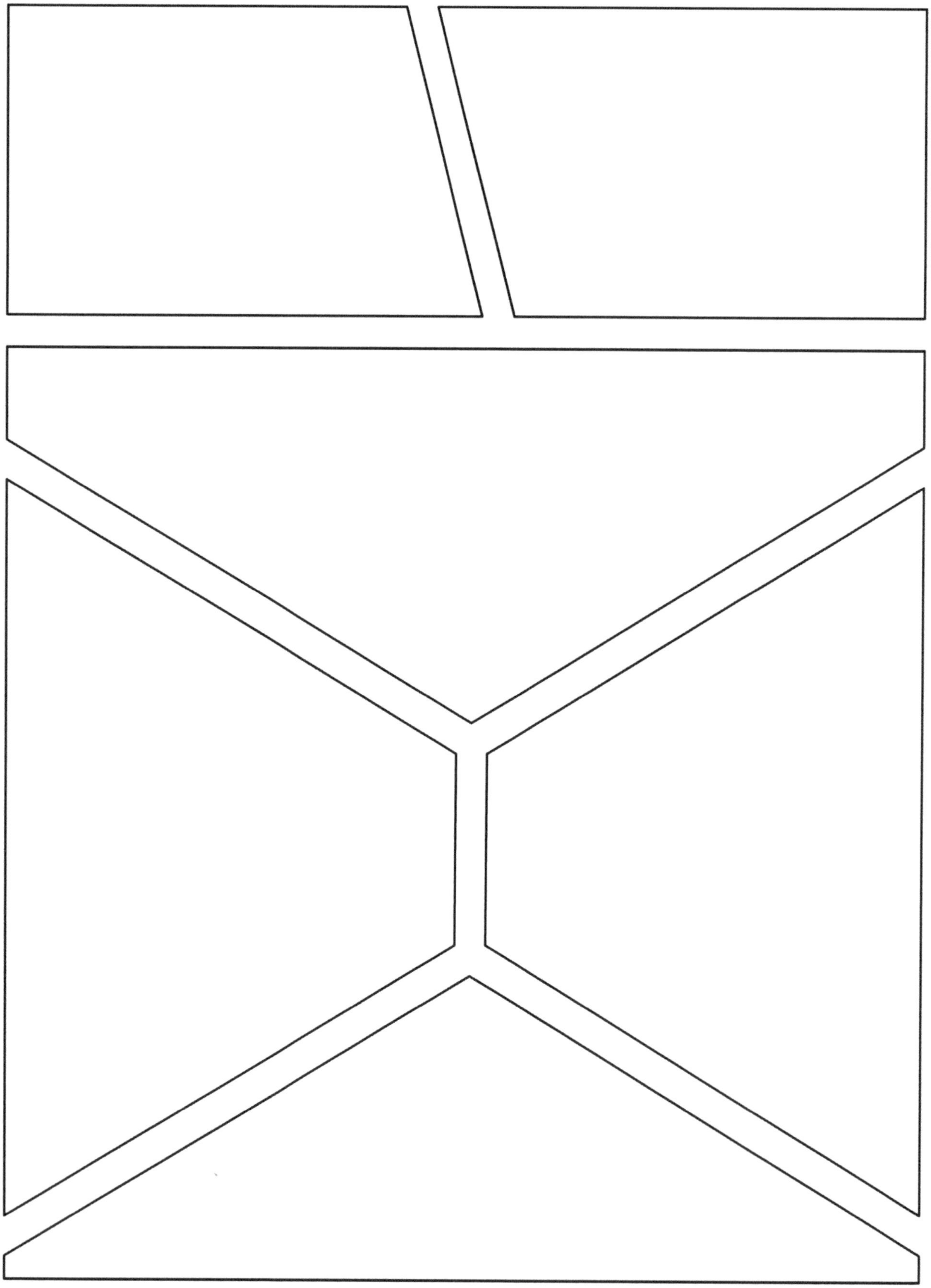

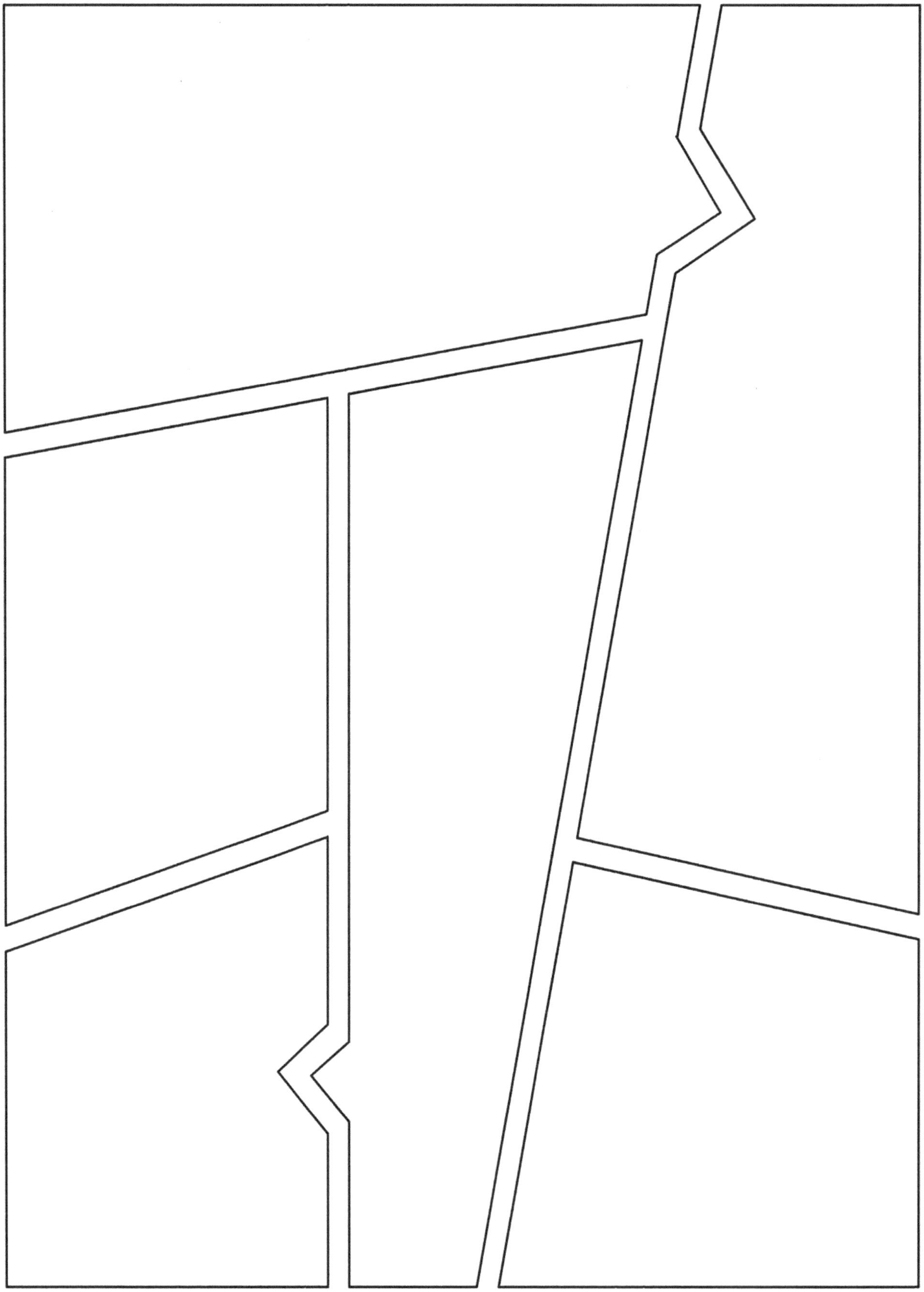

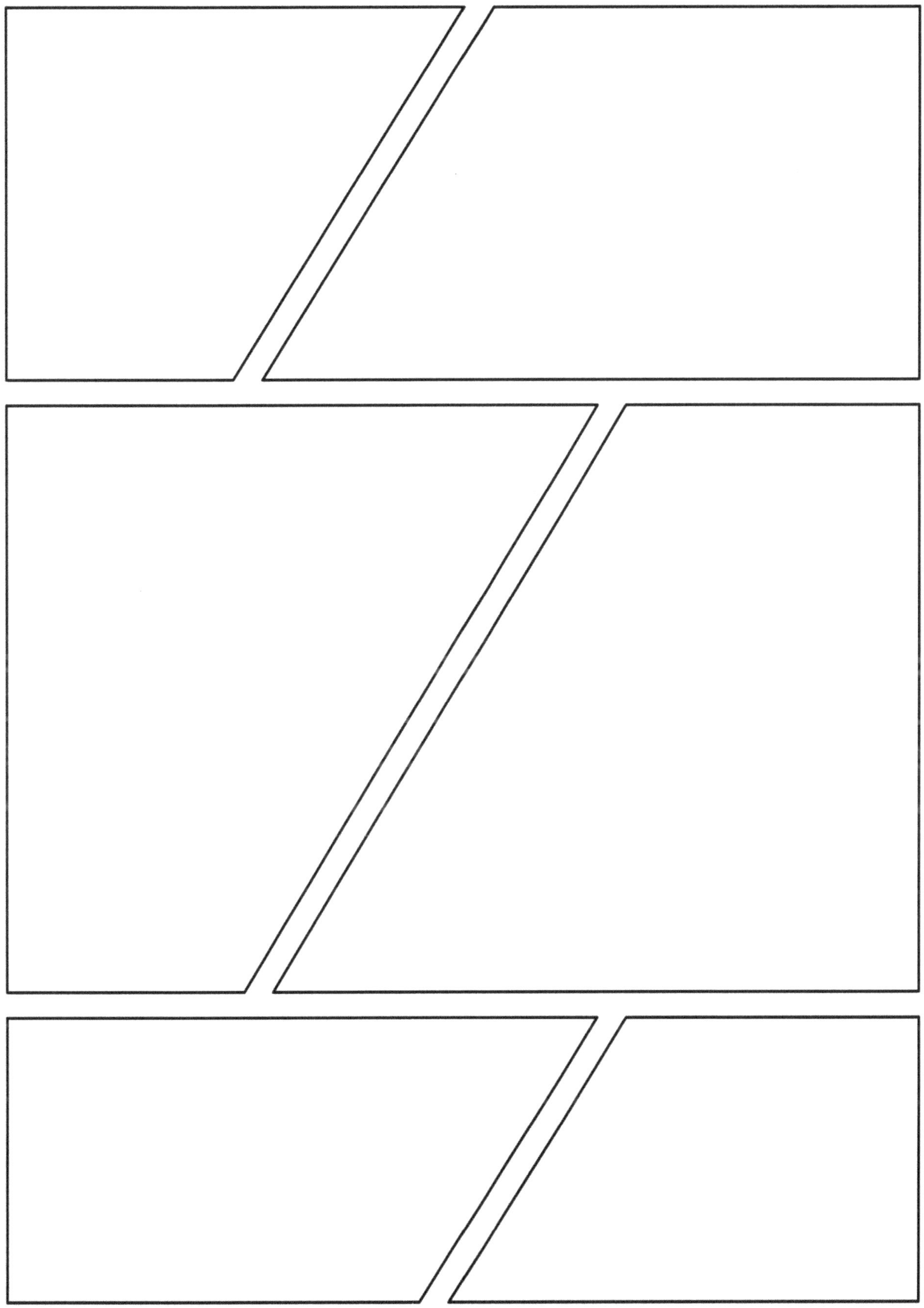

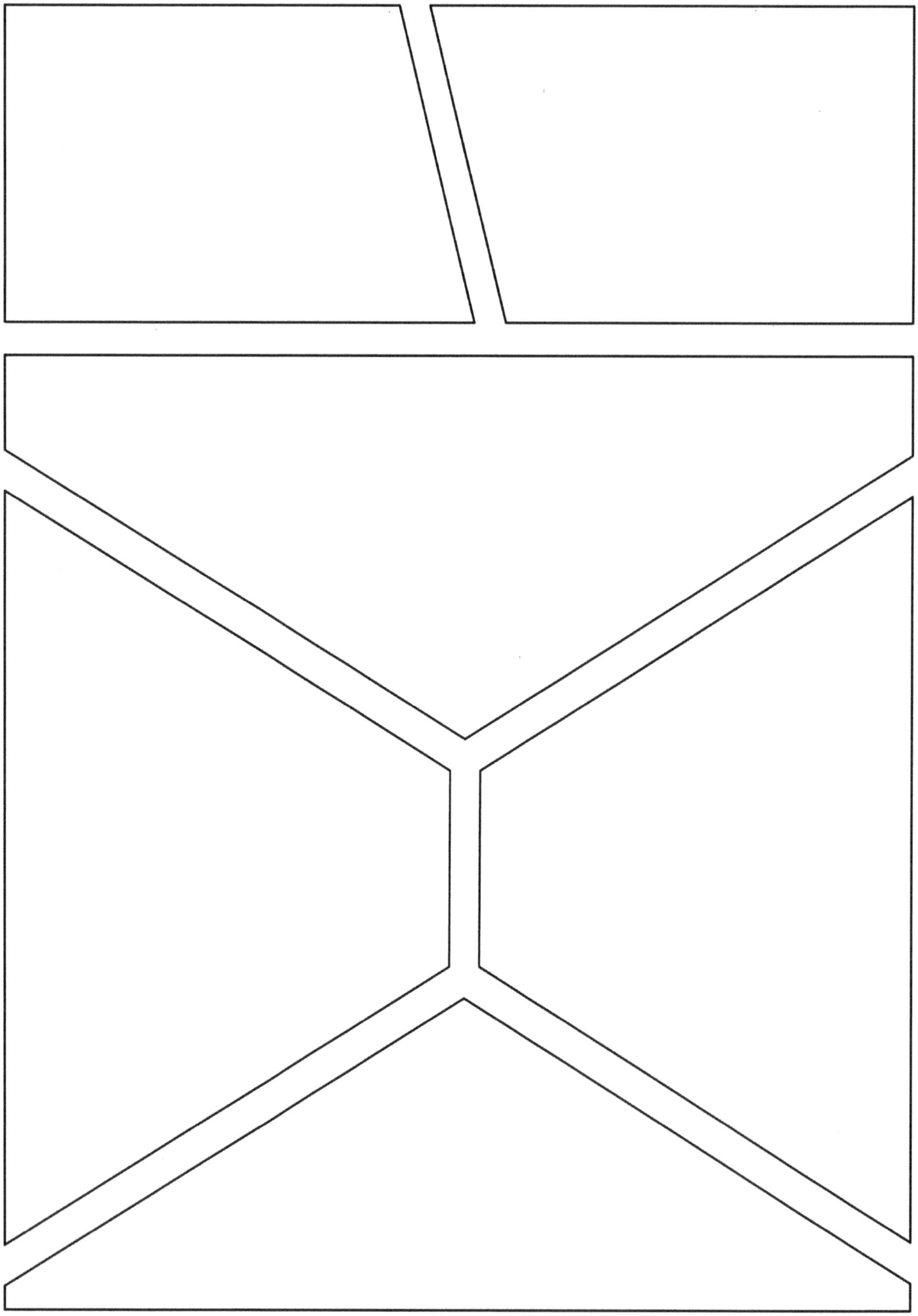

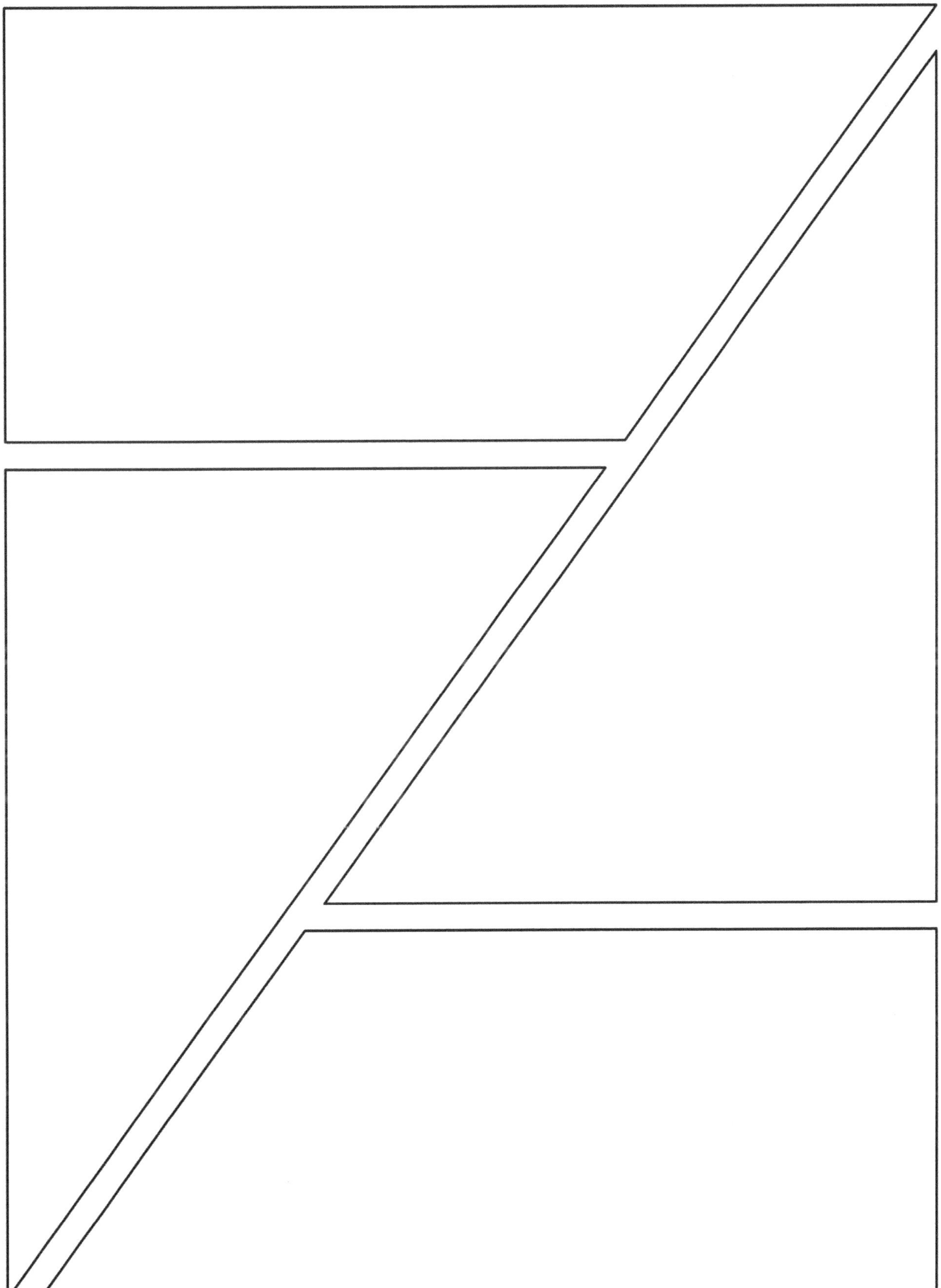

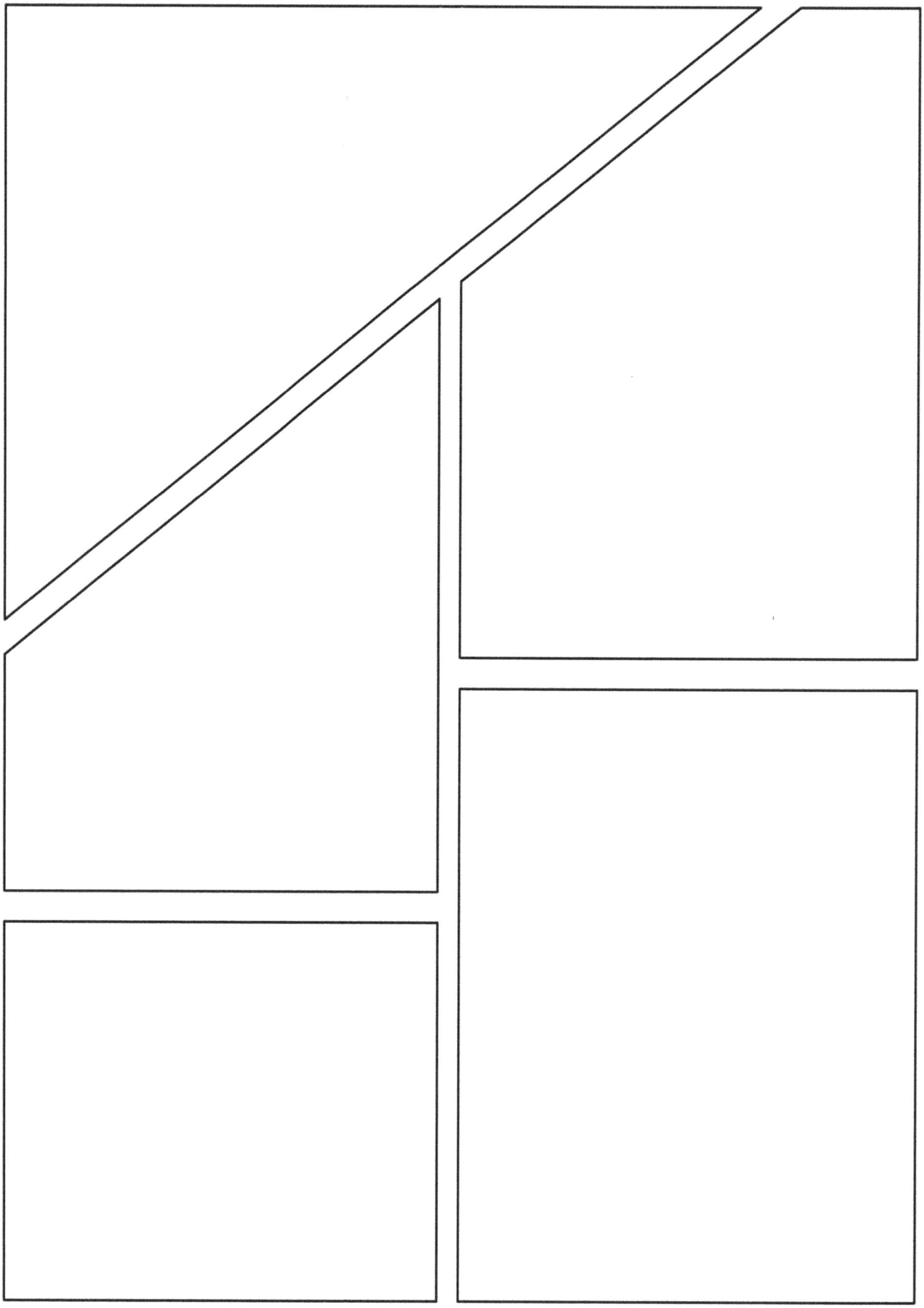

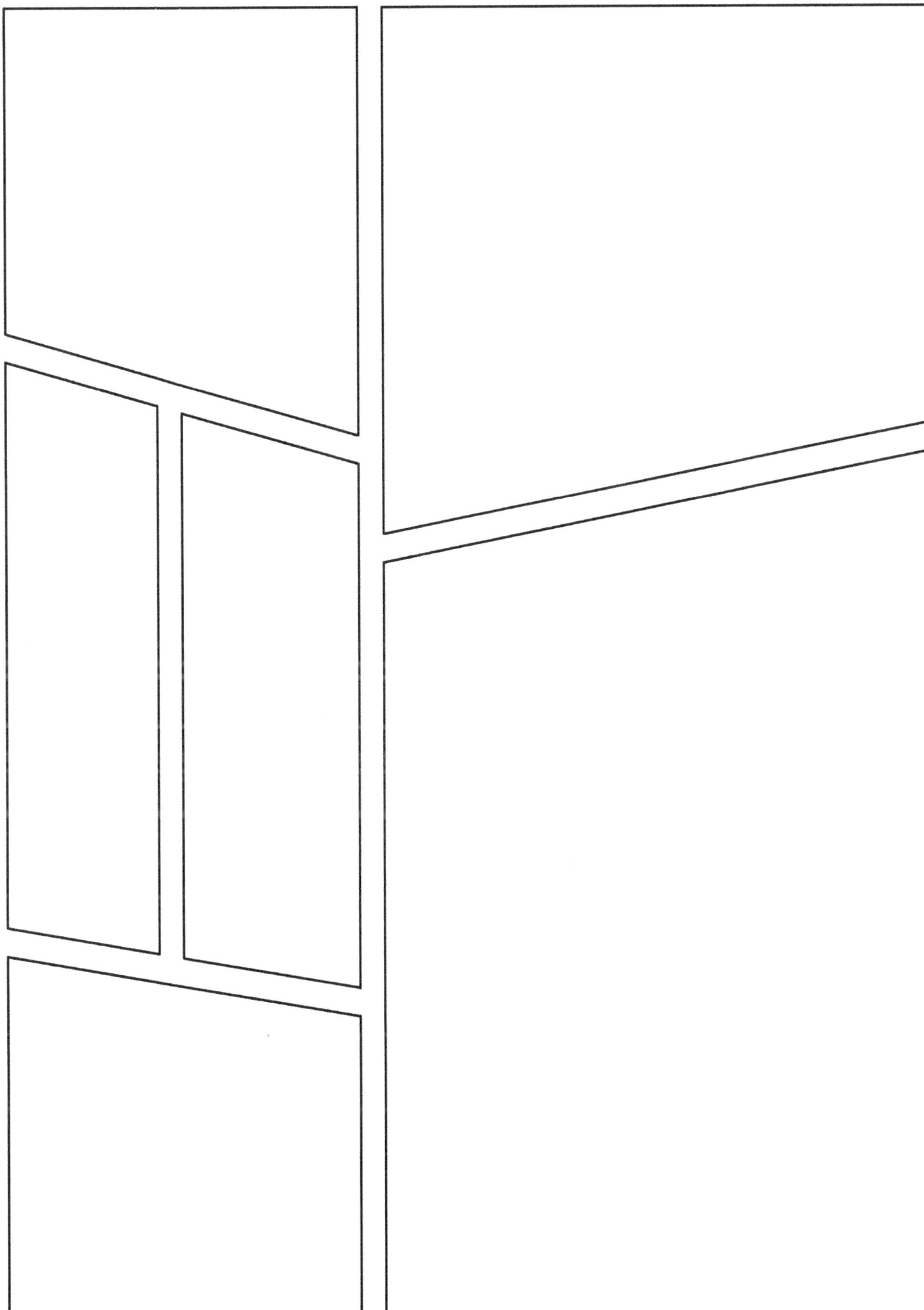

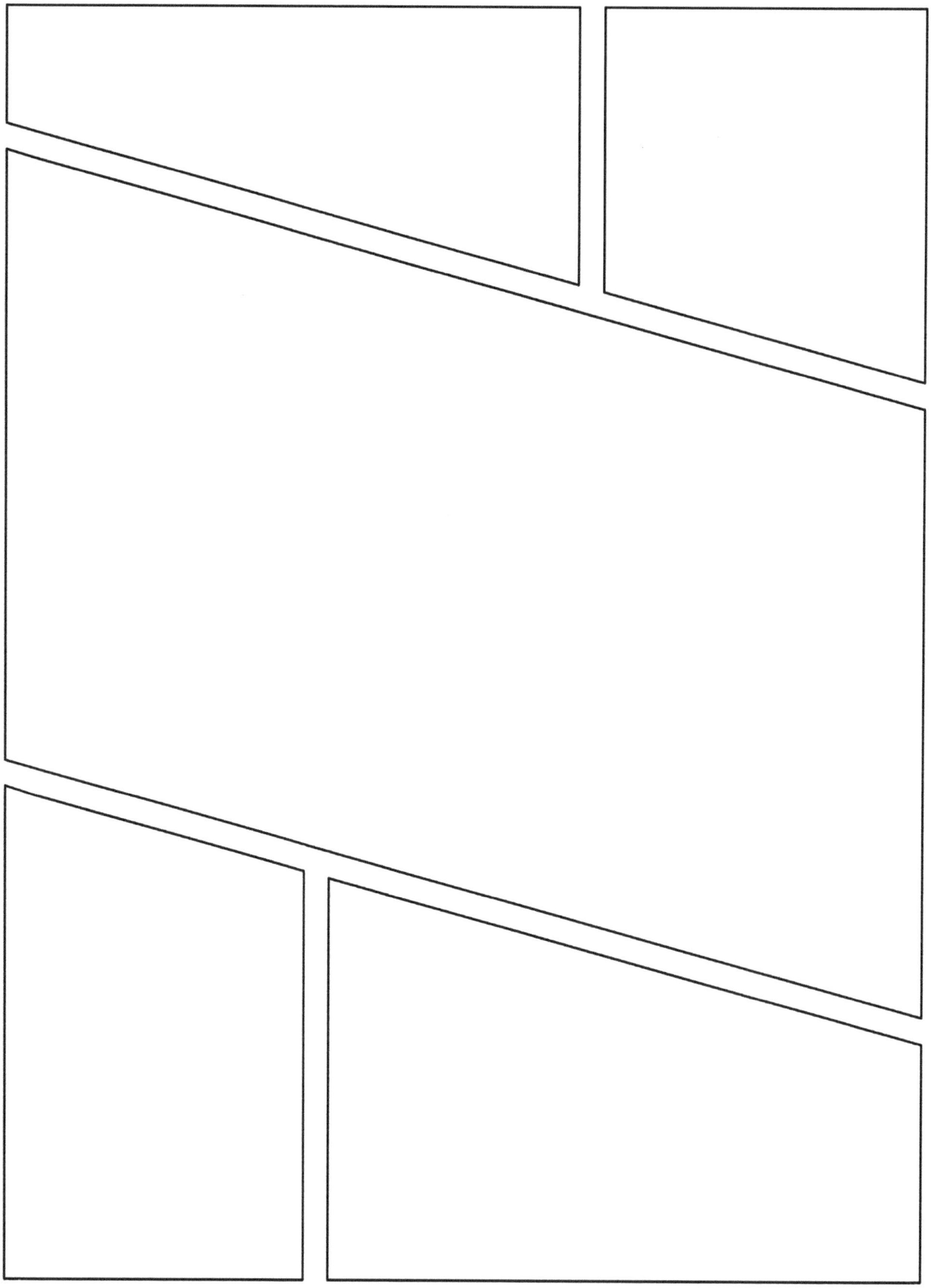

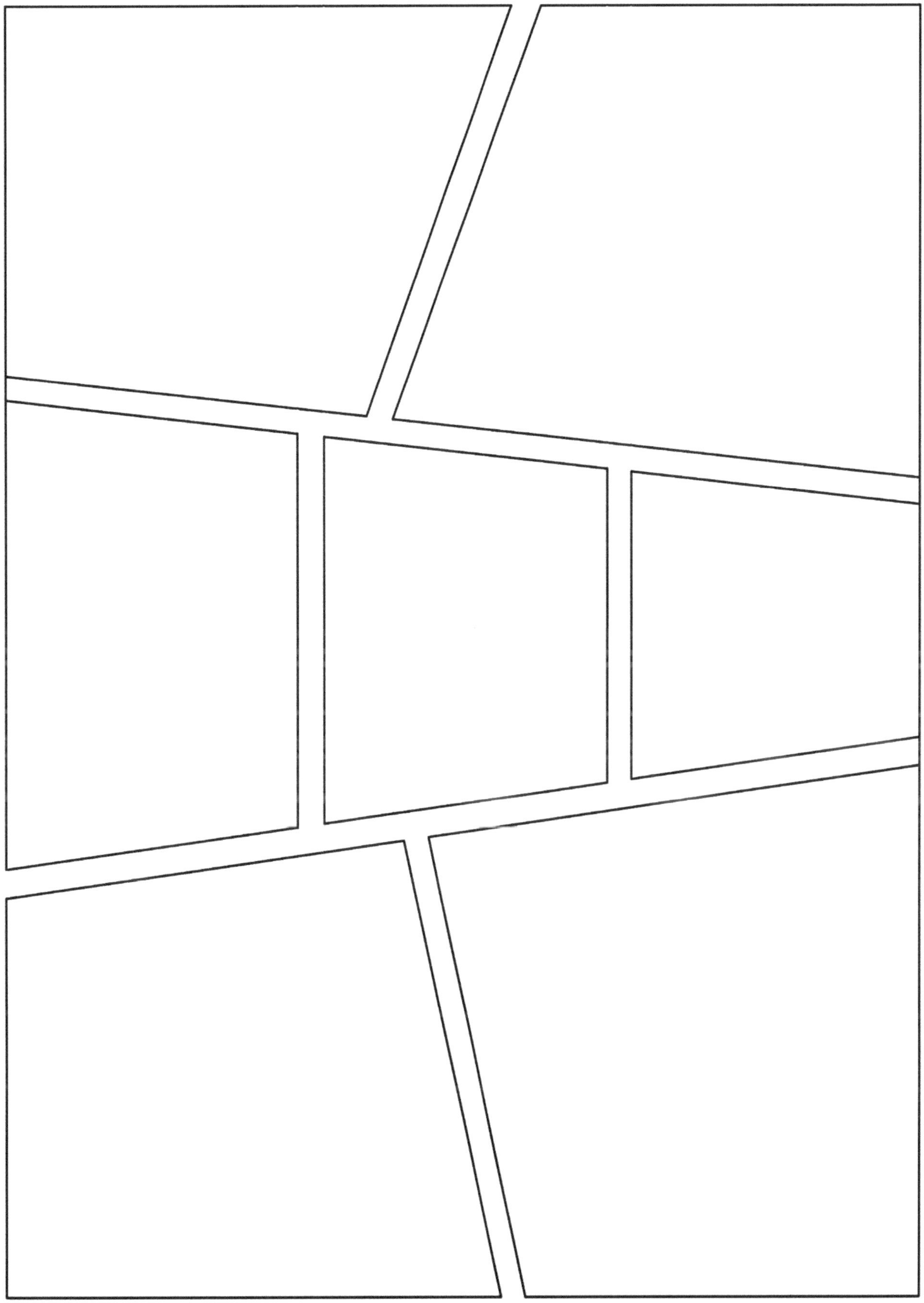

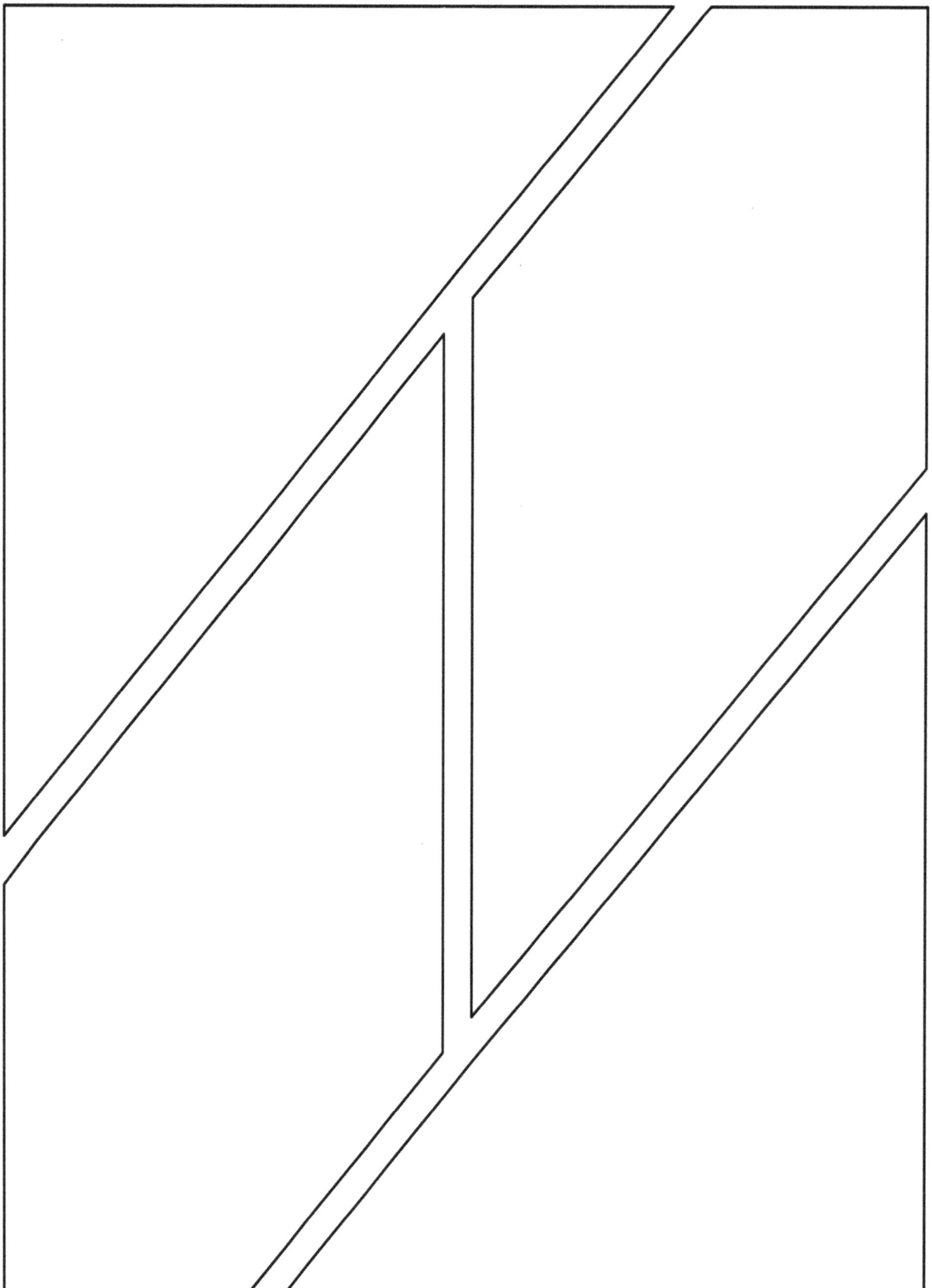

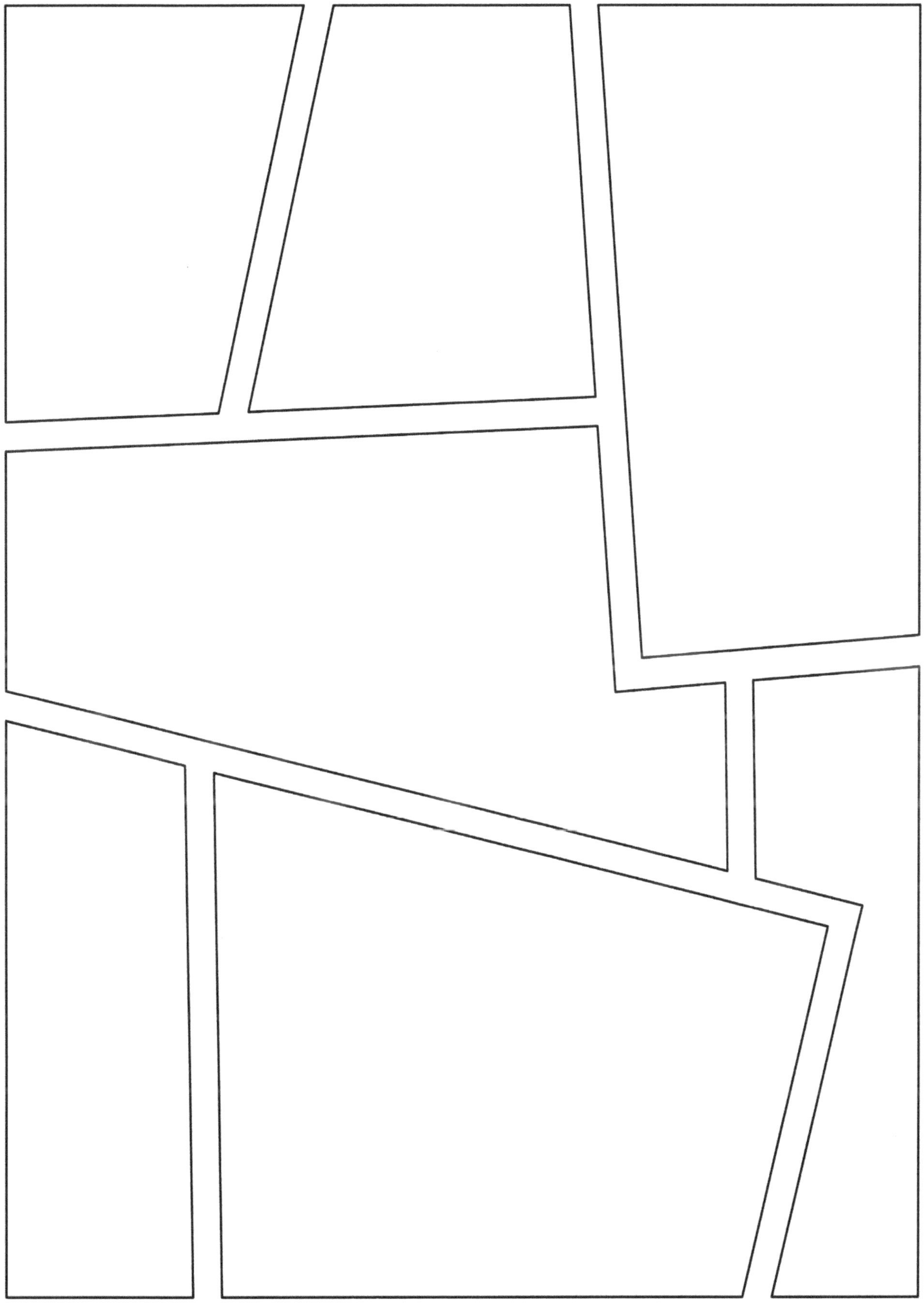

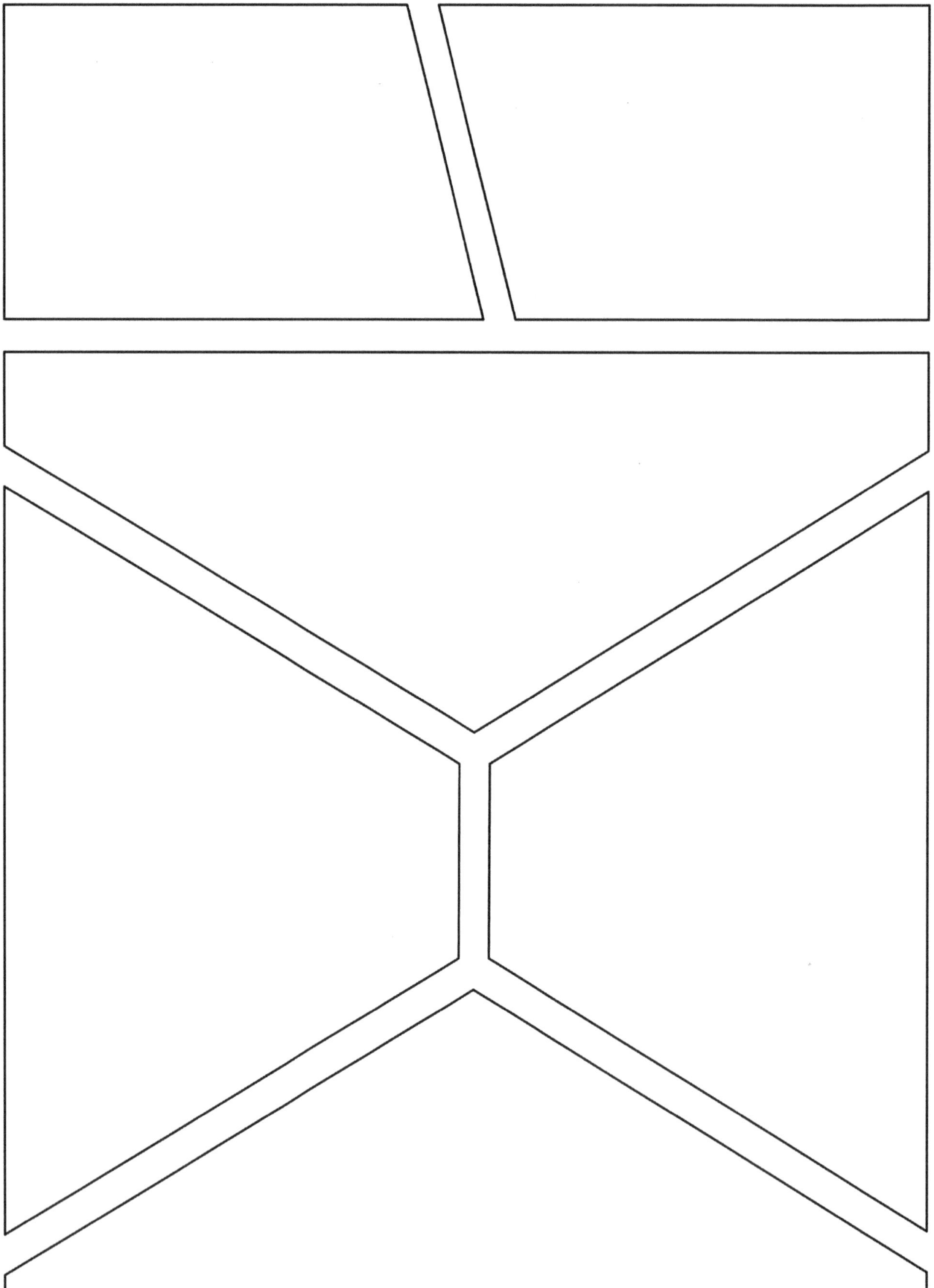

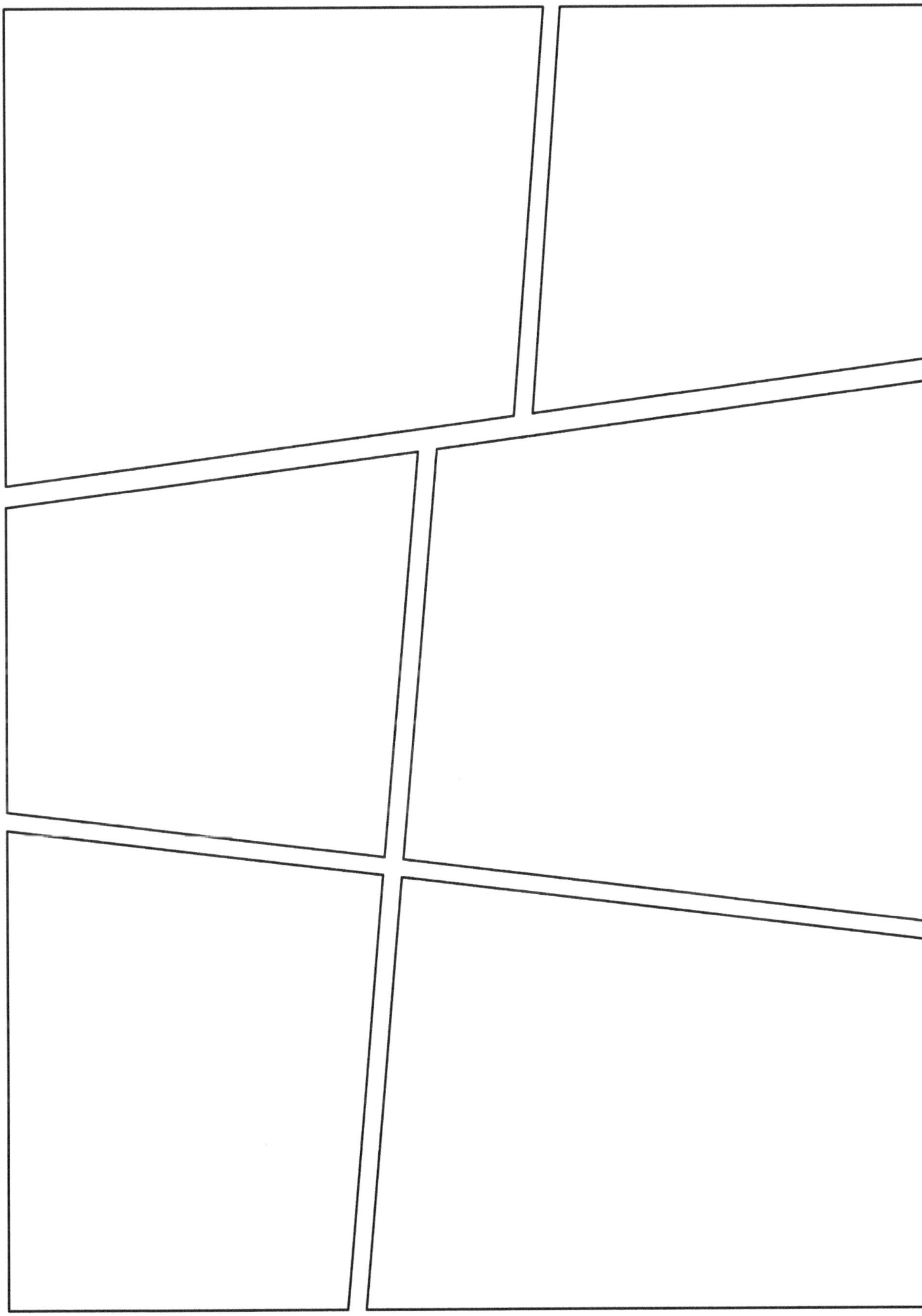

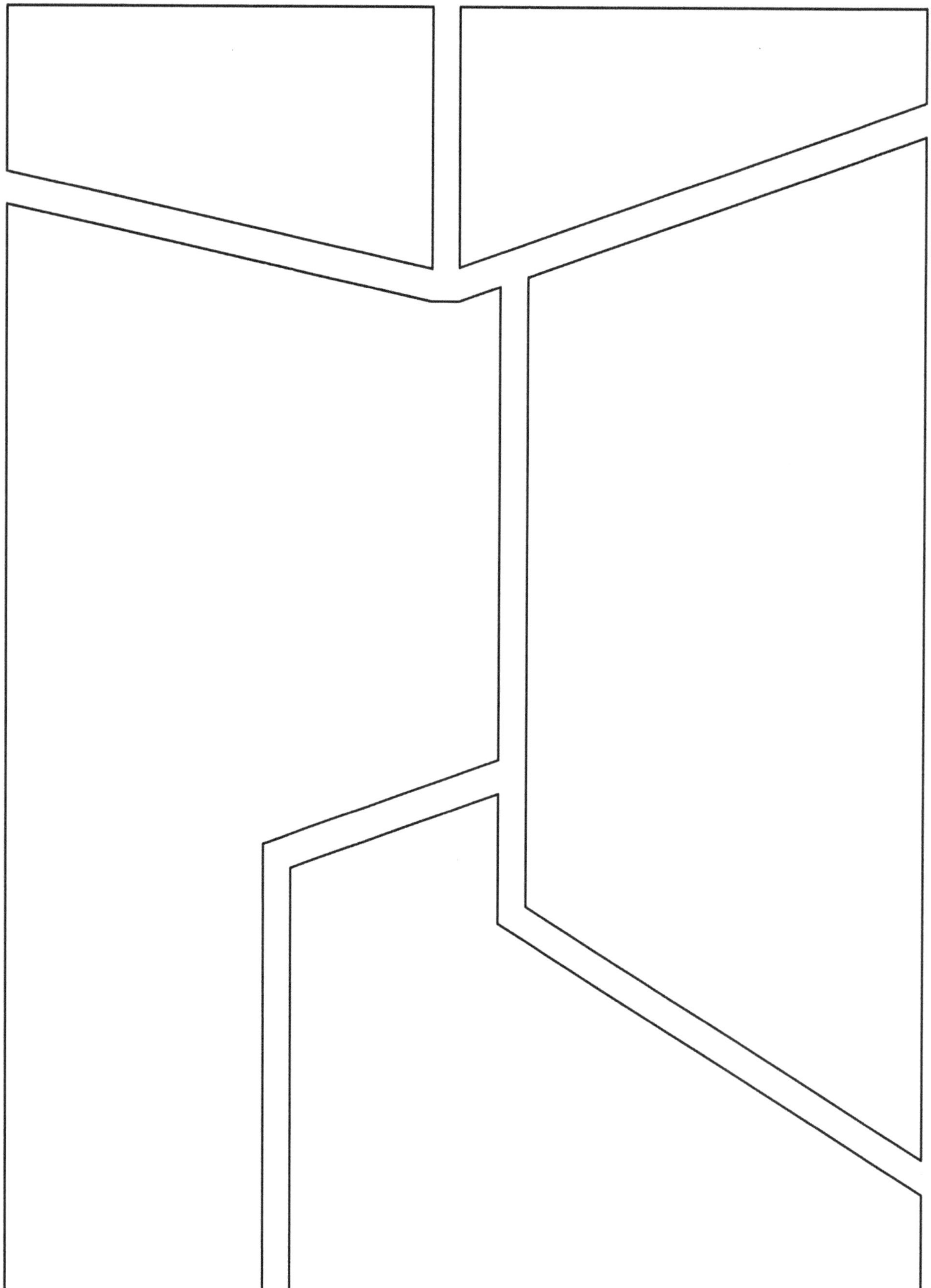

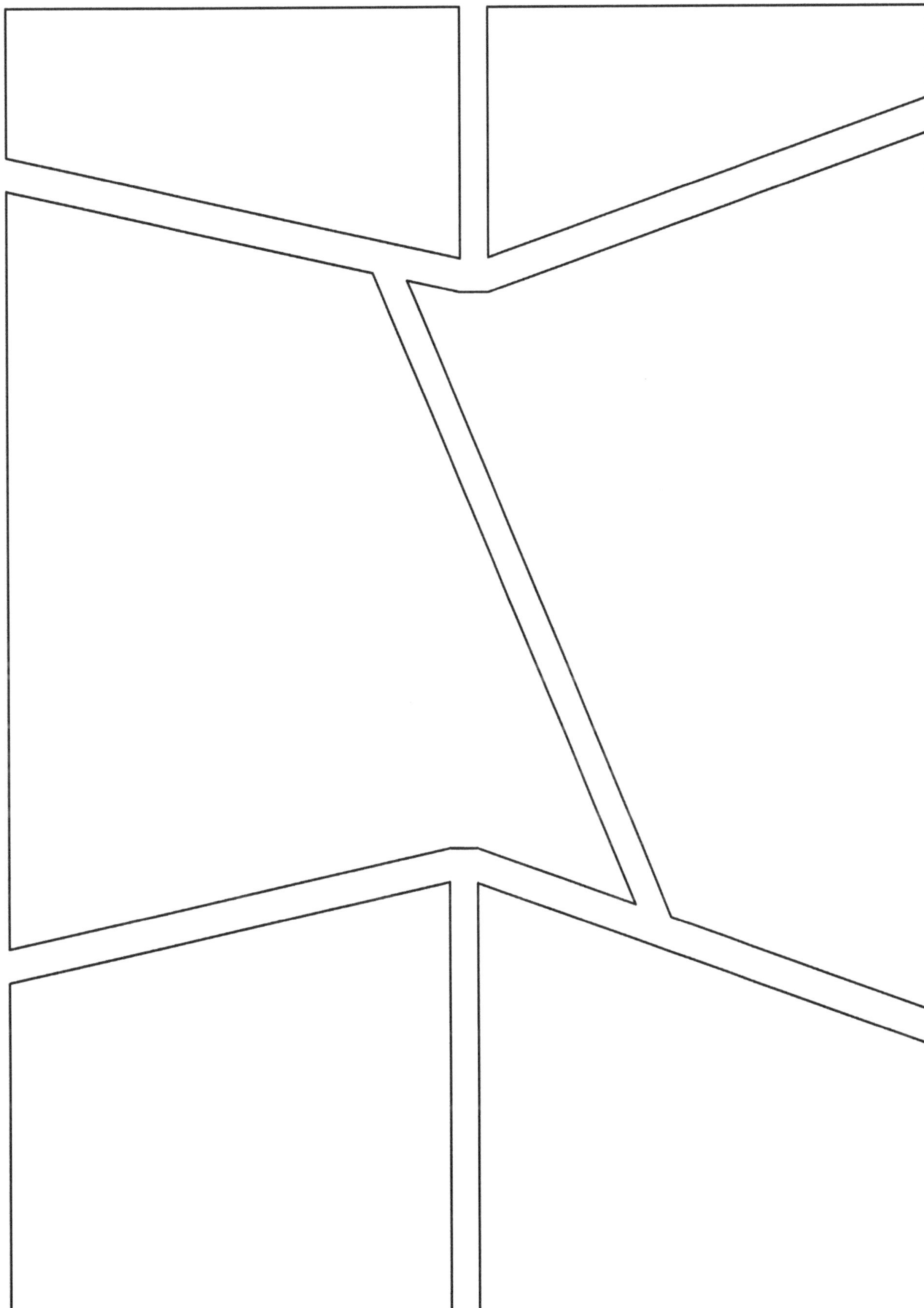

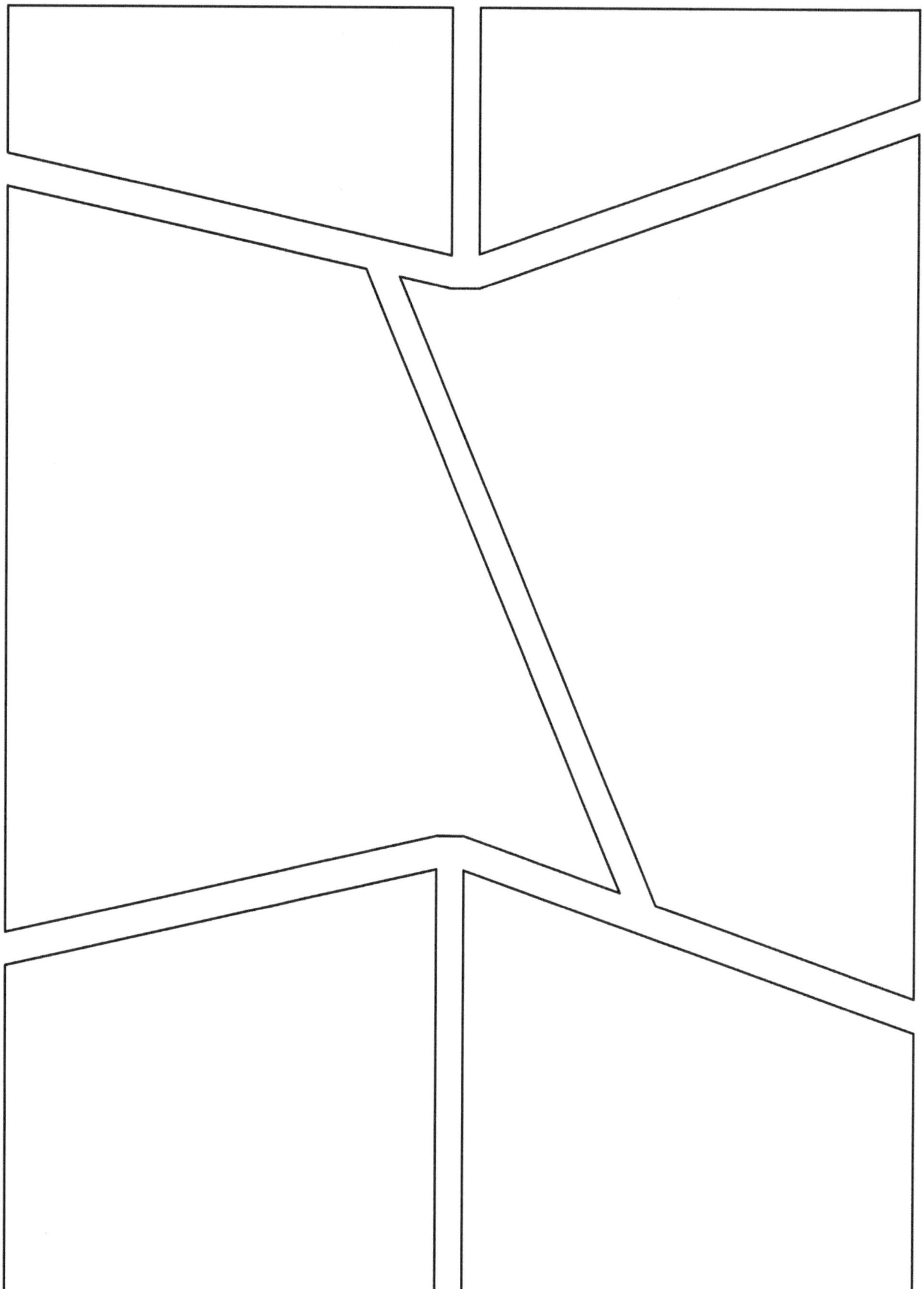

About the Author

Kaye Nutman, a UK/Aussie living in Melbourne, has also written a children's novella for ages 8-12 years called 'The Truth About Amber' – 'When Little Fibs Turn into Great Big Lies'. It is set in Utah, USA. You will find it in many places including her author website at https://kayenutman.com It is available as an eBook too!

That's not all! She is a hybrid writer of fiction and non-fiction books too.

Kaye has a Facebook group - Kaye Nutman – Author. She'd ***love*** you to go and join up to hear about her next set of Comic and Graphic Novel Blank Books, her other books, and more!

The Truth about Amber has a cartoon style illustration at the beginning of each of its twelve chapters, showcasing the fabulous and whacky characters.

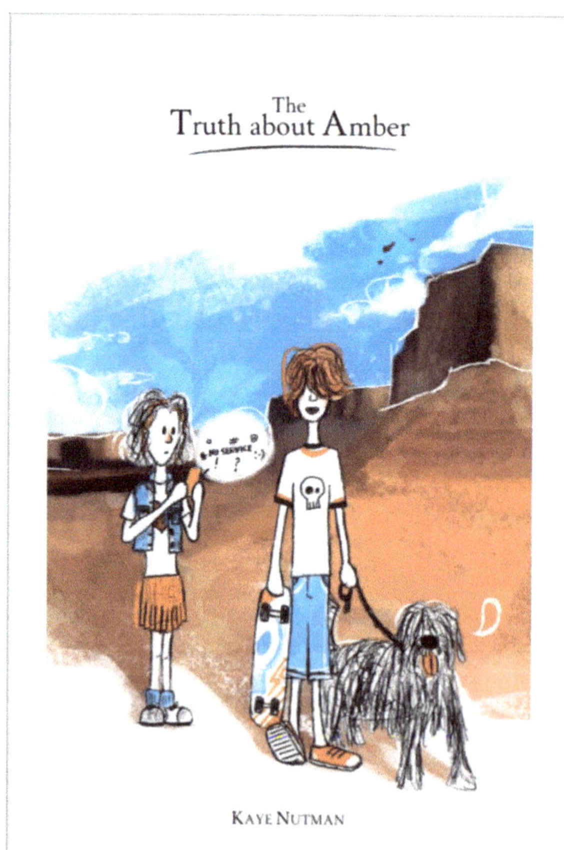

The cast of characters from 'The Truth About Amber'

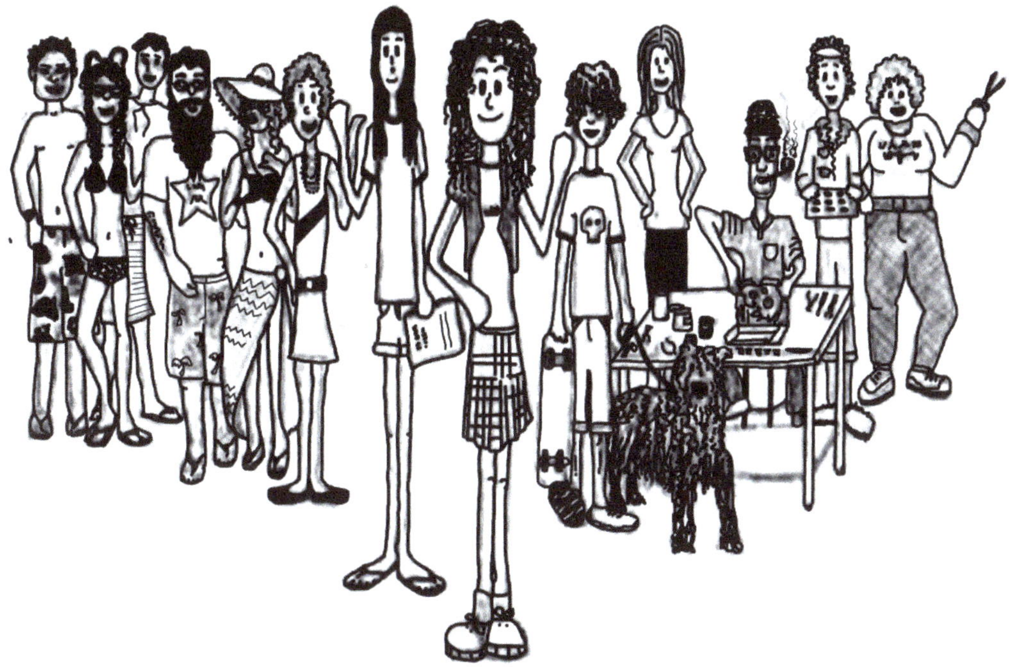

HEY, LOVERS OF COMIC STRIP DRAWING!

Did you enjoy making your own graphic novel? Isn't it FUN?
I'd love to hear what you thought about this book.
Did you like the way it was laid out?
Were there plenty of sketch pages?
Enough panels?
Were the 'A Few Things to Think About' pages helpful?
What else did you like?

Please consider leaving a review wherever you bought this book.
It helps so much!
If you have something nice to say I'd love to know what it is!
You can also contact me through my website:
www.kayenutman-writer.com

★★★★★

Speech Bubbles

Cut Out, Write on, and Paste into your Graphic Novel panels

Cut Out, Write on, and Paste into your Graphic Novel panels

www.ingramcontent.com/pod-product-compliance
Ingram Content Group UK Ltd.
Pitfield, Milton Keynes, MK11 3LW, UK
UKHW061134310726
14090UKWH00038B/1425

9 780987 640444